What Does the Bible Say About Demons?

A Styled Demonology

by Ken Ammi

What is thy name?
And he answered, saying,
My name is Legion: for we are many.
—Mark 5:9

No End Books

"…of making many books there is no end;
and much study is a weariness of the flesh.
Let us hear the conclusion of the whole matter:
Fear God, and keep his commandments:
for this is the whole duty of man."
—Ecclesiastes 12

"Through his writings on the paranormal in the Bible,
Ken Ammi offers insights based on meticulous research"
—Josh Peck, author of *Cherubim Chariots:
Exploring the Extradimensional Hypothesis*

"Great job! Very well researched!"
—Dr. Heather Lynn, archeologist and
author of *Land of the Watchers*

Introduction

Hereinafter is presented my best attempt at preseting that which the titled promises, *What Does the Bible Say About Demons?*, in an unbiased as possible manner—including entities related to the general topic of demons.

Yes, the title also include *A Styled Demonology* and it is at the ology portion, which dentotes systemization, when an elucidator is generally forced to speculate to whatever degree. And, I, at least, seek to make those speculations obvious— meaning that it should be evident to the reader when the speculations are being proposed—and seeks to keep the speculations as close to what the texts are clearly stating as possible.

But why speculate at all? Well, certainly one could publish a text in a just the facts maam manner such a nothing but bulletpointed quotations and citations.

Yet, the above referenced systemization comes into play when seeking to comprehend what is being told to us such as: how does fact A connect to fact B, C, D, etc.
Also, the above referenced speculation comes into play because the connection between, say, A and B may not be evident and in fact, may be unknown.

Some unknowns as simply due to the fact that as exampled by this case, the Bible is not a text about Angles as a main focus and so we are told certain things about them but the Bible is not meant to be an *everything you wanted to know about demons and related entities* sort of text.

Please note that the majority of that which we know about demons is based on common knowledge. Problematically however, common knowledge are those things that everybody knows even though nobody knows how anyone knows.

At least when it comes to the Bible's statements about demons, you may find that your views on everything from what demons are to how the behave and whether they have distinct personalities.

Lastly, speaking of systemization: this gets more complex—as well as more fascinating and rewarding—since the issue of demons and related entities in the Bible does not exist in a vacuum but connects with issues that you will find covered in the companion to this text which are as follows and of which this volume is the conclusion:
What Does the Bible Say About Angels? A Styled Angelology
What Does the Bible Say About the Devil Satan? A Styled Satanology
What Does the Bible Say About Various Paranormal Entities? A Styled Paranormology
What Does the Bible Say About Giants? A Styled Giantology

In essence, there is God and there are Earthdwellers such as human, animals, insects, etc. and yet, the Bible presents a plethora of beings who inhabint an inbetween realm: this series seeks to elucidate that which the Bible tells us regarding all such beings.

Table of Contents

Demons, Devils and Spirits

As will be considered herein, it appears safe to assume that no more Angels fell after the Genesis 6 affair. Some reasoning on the matter appears warranted before moving on. There seems to be a correlation between Angels and humans. Humans experience one lifespan upon the Earth and it is only within this lifespan that they are either saved or lost; forgiven or fallen as in eternally.

Angels also seem to have had allotted to them a specific amount of time during which some of them fell and some did not. The fall was eternally solidified for the fallen just as was the loyalty of the others. One thing to note is that "everlasting fire" is "prepared for the devil and his Angels" (Matthew 25:4).

This means firstly, that everlasting fire was prepared for being for whom the question of God's existence was a non-issue; they did not have to wonder, guess or philosophize but knew it with one hundred percent certainty.
Yet, of course, Romans 1 states "that which may be known of God is manifest in them; for God hath shewed *it* unto them. For the invisible things of him from the creation of the world are clearly seen, being understood by the things that are made, *even* his eternal power and Godhead; so that they are without excuse."
Secondly, it means that their rebellion, their fall, carried along with it eternal consequences.

5

Also, there is simply no biblical indication that any other or more Angels fell at any time but during the Genesis 6 affair (there is a difference between a *fall* such as per Genesis 6 and a *casting out* as per Revelation 12 and only those who fell are cast out).

Keep in mind that the one third of Angels (*stars* symbolically: also see Daniel 8:10) that the dragon causes to be cast out of heaven in the heavenly war mentioned in Revelation are the very ones that have been incarcerated since their fall during the Genesis 6 affair. Between their fall and being cast out they are released and wreak havoc upon the Earth as per Revelation 9.

If, as appears to be the case, the fallen sons of God Angels are safely locked away and no more Angels fell or will fall and, additionally, if Satan is the only Cherub that fell and no Seraphim fell; who has been wreaking such havoc upon the Earth via the spiritual realm in the meantime?

Beyond the obvious answer that it is Satan is the question as to how Satan is going about doing so and the answer to that question is; through Satan's administration who are, generically speaking, the demons.
But, pray tell, who or what are demons?

What Are Demons?

The Bible does not seem to specifically identify who or what demons are. Note also that as is considered below; there are many terms for malevolent paranormal beings.
These terms may refer to the same beings in a manner which denotes different ranks, abilities, etc. or they may simply be interchangeable (which often seems to be the case).

Within this section two theories will be elucidated as to what demons are (the term *demon* is being employed here because it seems to be the most recognizable common parlance term for malevolent paranormal beings). The two theories are *demons are not fallen Angels* and *demons are fallen Angels*.

Demons are Not Fallen Angels

Many identify demons as fallen Angels and yet, or so it seems, they do so without any biblical foundation. It is a common assumption and the sort of common knowledge that everyone knows even though no one seems to know how or why everyone knows it.

If all of the fallen Angels are incarcerated then demons cannot be fallen Angels. Moreover, on the view that Angels inhabit the equivalent of *glorified bodies* another relevant question is how could they possess human bodies?

Of course, Jesus inhabits a glorified resurrection body and also lives within believers (see John 6:56 & 14:17; Ephesians 3:17; Colossians 1:27) yet, He is God, He is omnipresent (see Matthew 18:20 & 28:20; John 1:47-48, 3:13) and Angels are not.

Recall what was noted in the preface about putting together puzzle pieces when dealing with such abstract concept about which we are not given many details. We can borrow a concept from the apocryphal texts generically known as the Book of Enoch (aka *1 Enoch* aka *Ethiopic Enoch* dating to circa 200 BC) that does not contradict the Bible (at least not on this one point, it does contradict the Bible on other points (see the *Wherein the Book of Enoch contradicts the Bible* section of my book *In Consideration of the Book(s) of Enoch*) and also makes sense. It seems to work as an explanatory identification of demons but then again, it does not.

Enoch 15:8-12 notes (R.H. Charles' 1917 AD translation):

> And now, the giants, who are produced from the spirits and flesh, shall be called evil spirits upon the earth, and on the earth shall be their dwelling.
>
> Evil spirits have proceeded from their bodies; because they are born from men, [[and]] from the holy Watchers is their beginning and primal origin; [they shall be evil spirits on earth, and] evil spirits shall they be called. [As for the spirits of heaven, in heaven shall be their dwelling, but as for the spirits of the earth which were born upon the

earth, on the earth shall be their
dwelling.]

And the spirits of the giants afflict,
oppress, destroy, attack, do battle,
and work destruction on the earth,
and cause trouble: they take no food,
[but nevertheless hunger] and thirst,
and cause offences. And these spirits
shall rise up against the children of
men and against the women, because
they have proceeded [from them].

There is much debate concerning the definition of
the term *nephiyl*. Strong's defines it as "properly, a
feller, i.e. a bully or tyrant:—giant." When assumed
to have its roots in Hebrew it is thought to come
from *naphal* (Strong's H5307) which is "A
primitive root; *to fall*, in a great variety of
applications...cast (down, self, [lots], out), cease,
die, divide (by lot), (let) fail, (cause to, let, make,
ready to) fall (away, down...overthrow, overwhelm,
perish, present (-ed, -ing), (make to) rot, slay, smite
out, X surely, throw down."

In turn, *naphal* is the primitive root of *nephel*
(Strong's H5309) which refers to "something fallen,
i.e. an abortion:—untimely birth" (Job 3:16, Psalm
58:8 and Ecclesiastes 6:3).

However, it appears more likely that the term
nephiyl derives from the Aramaic root *naphiyla*
which means *giant* (for an elucidation of what *giant*
means, see the *Codex Giganticus* section of *What
Does the Bible Say About Giants?*).

As just seen, Enoch employs the term as Watchers, *'iyr* (Strong's H5894) as elucidated within *The Watcher Texts* section of *What Does the Bible Say About Various Paranormal Entities?*.

To reiterate, the Enoch claim does not contradict the Bible on this point and makes sense; since Angels are embodied, they inhabit bodies as do we, they could not *enter* the bodies of humans so as to possess them. The Enoch claim makes sense because it denotes the spirit of a previously embodied being seeking embodiment again.

Thus, the identification of and explanation for demons is coming along just fine and then—we run into God's platypus. When going about doing taxonomy within the field of biology it begins easily enough until you get to the platypus and note that it fits within various categories hence, not into any one neat and simple one.

Well, Satan is like God's platypus for as we seek to categorize him we note that, indeed, he is a Cherub but appears to be the only one who fell, but he was not involved in the Genesis 6 affair with the Angels, he is not incarcerated as they are, he reported to God regarding his activities, etc.

In any regard, the point of bringing this up is that we are just about to conclude that yes indeed, the spirit of a previously embodied beings seeking embodiment again makes sense but then we run into Luke 22:3 that states, "Then entered Satan into Judas…"

Satan does not seem to be a disembodied spirit and the bodies of Cherubim are described as noted in *The Cherub Texts* section of *What Does the Bible Say About Various Paranormal Entities?*. While they are generally seen in visions (such as by Ezekiel) and are made into sculpted and carved figures (see Exodus 25:18-20, 37:7-9; 1 Kings 6, 2 Chronicles 3, 5:7-8), the fact is that Cherubim were stationed on Earth to guard the way into the Garden of Eden and were thus, physically present.

Then again, this is highly speculative as we are not specifically told anywhere in the Bible but perhaps Satan's body was destroyed, leaving him a disembodied spirt. Isaiah 14 states:

> How art thou fallen from heaven, O Lucifer, son of the morning! how art thou cut down to the ground…thou shalt be brought down to hell, to the sides of the pit…thou art cast out of thy grave like an abominable branch, and as the raiment of those that are slain, thrust through with a sword, that go down to the stones of the pit; as a carcase trodden under feet. Thou shalt not be joined with them in burial…

Ezekiel 28 states:

> I will cast thee to the ground…I bring forth a fire from the midst of thee, it shall devour thee, and I will bring thee to ashes upon the earth…thou shalt be a terror, and never shalt thou be any more…

Of course, this may all be indicative of his final destruction after the millennial reign.

Satan is said to have *entered* into Judas just as the *daimonion* who possessed the *Gergesene/Gadarene* man entered into the swine.

However, there may not be a *real* problem at all as the word for enter in such instances is *eiserchomai* (Strong's G1525) which is "to *enter* (literally or figuratively): - X arise, come (in, into), enter in (-to), go in (through)." A word that comes from two others namely, *eis* (Strong's G1519) that is, "A primary preposition; *to* or *into*...expressing motion (literally or figuratively)" and *erchomai* (Strong's G2064) as in "to come or go (in a great variety of applications, literally and figuratively): - accompany, appear, bring, come enter, fall out, go, grow, X light, X next, pass, resort, be set."

That the definition of these three words all note that to enter is employed literally or figuratively means that there may not be a problem at all with the Enoch statements on demons and the biblical statements on Satan entering into Judas.

It seems proper to identify the various daimonion who went out of one body and entered others as literal. This is because the man was exhibiting symptoms of being possessed, then the daimonion are said to have left him and entered into the swine, the swine ran, plunged into the waters, drowned and then the man is said to regain his wits, etc.

It may then be proper to identify Satan entering Judas as figurative. While we do not know very much about Judas, we do know that he would steal from the common purse that he, Jesus and the Apostles shared (John 12:6), that he betrayed Jesus (Matthew 10:4, et al.) and never was a believer as John 6:64 seems to imply, "…Jesus knew from the beginning who they were that believed not, and who should betray him."

Note that 1 John 2:19 specifies that "They went out from us, but they were not of us; for if they had been of us, they would *no doubt* have continued with us: but *they went out*, that they might be made manifest that they were not all of us."

This means that he was opened to evil influence as he was both unrepentant and very much aware of the Messiah's appearance and ministry. Also, after Satan entered him, he does not exhibit symptoms of possession but only of evil influence.

I could have simply been asserted a simple, affirmative, reference to the Book of Enoch's identification and explanation for demons. However, it is important to elucidate the matter as much as it can be for the sake of working through potential difficulties.

It may also be important to note that demons are often noted to cause physical ailments of various sorts. However, the Bible does not envisage that any and all illnesses are the result of demonism. For example, Leviticus 13 outlines a very advanced medical procedure whereby to observe and diagnose leprosy which includes quarantine, how to dispose of items identifies as being contaminated, etc. This is done without any reference to demonic possession or influence whatsoever.

This is the case even though people with such ailments were generally considered ritually unclean (part of the quarantine concept) and would perform cleansing rituals if and when they regained their health (part of the process of avoiding spreading contagions).

Yet, the ultimate and biblical explanation for how Satan "entered" into Judas seems to come from recalling that Satan is a Cherub.

Ezekiel 10:17 describes the Cherubim as *the living creatures* and in referring to their interaction with the wheels within wheels it states, "When they stood, these stood; and when they were lifted up, these lifted up themselves also: for the spirit of the living creature was in them" (for details, see *The Cherub Texts* section of *What Does the Bible Say About Various Paranormal Entities?*).

Think for example, about how in our day a drone pilot does not actually enter into the drone physically so as to pilot it from within. Rather, they control the drone from without as they can do so from many, many miles away from the drone.

In this way, we can understand what it means for the mind, intention, etc. of someone being within, guiding, moving, etc. something or someone else. In the case of the pilot: the human's mind is linked to the drone via high tech. In the case of the Cherubim: their spirit somehow enters the wheels.

Thus, just as "the spirit of the living creature was in" the wheels, Satan's spirit was in Judas.

Demons are Fallen Angels

The, likely new, theory that will now be proposed which seeks to identify and define demons will require a circumlocution, so just stick with it (or, as this theory develops through a few pages; you can go to the end of this section, consider the succinctly stated conclusion and then, if interested, come back and read the development).

The claim that demons are fallen Angels is commonly held and yet seems to be mostly based on the rhetorical question, "Well, what else could they be?" Thus, this is actually not a new theory but is more specifically the probable mechanism which may explain the claim that demons are fallen Angels.

Within the *Sons of God* section of *What Does the Bible Say About Angels?*, Revelation 9 was considered and will be again herein within the context of seeking to identify and define *demons*:

> ...I [John] saw a star fall from
> heaven unto the Earth...And he
> opened the bottomless pit; and there
> arose a smoke out of the pit, as the
> smoke of a great furnace; and the sun
> and the air were darkened by reason
> of the smoke of the pit. And there
> came out of the smoke locusts upon
> the Earth...

The deeply symbolic description of this event begins by describing those that exit the bottomless pit as locusts. Note that the bottomless pit is the Abyss in which the fallen *song of God* Angels were incarcerated due to the Genesis 6 affair.

The symbolic language refers to them having "power, as the scorpions…tails like unto scorpions," being like "horses prepared unto battle," having "crowns like gold" with "the faces of men" and "the hair of women" plus "teeth of lions" wearing "breastplates, as it were breastplates of iron" and that "sound of their wings was as the sound of chariots."

There may or may not be a manner whereby to track down every detail of the symbolic language yet, one thing is certain which is that what can be readily tracked down is very informative to our context.

From texts such as Nahum 3:15 it is readily discernable that locusts are being employed as symbolic of there being many, "make thyself many as the locusts" and in verse 17, as in Revelation 9, there is a reference to crows within the context of symbolic locusts, "Thy crowned are as the locusts." Crowns, of course, denote authority and thus, sovereignty.

Scorpions are obviously employed as symbolic of pain and death from being poisonously stung. And yet, there is more to it than that as Jesus correlates "serpents and scorpions" with "all the power of the enemy" which He is giving His followers the "power to tread on" (Luke 10:19).

While within Revelation there are various horses of various colors, they all represent movement as they are conveyances for key personages performing key tasks.

Thus, beyond more symbolic details; the main point is that out of the bottomless pit there arise many beings pertaining to the power of the enemy (that is, Satan). In one way or another; these beings are on Satan's side.

We are told that upon being released they wreak havoc on Earth "their power was to hurt men five months" and nothing more is said of them besides that their king is Abaddon/Apollyon. I contend that these are the very same Angels who are then referenced in Revelation 12 as engaging in a war in heaven.

Beyond Satan-Devil-Dragon-Serpent, the false prophet and the beast(s) there are virtually no references to demons, by any other name, within Revelation:
9:20 states "that they should not worship devils [*daimonion*], and idols…" and so this is not, necessarily, a reference to beings but to those who would worship them with a correlation to idolatrous images.

16:13 has John stating, "I saw three unclean spirits [*akathartos pneuma*] like frogs come out of the mouth of the dragon, and out of the mouth of the beast, and out of the mouth of the false prophet" which means that these are either unique non-typical demon-like beings or typical demons that resided within very special characters.

16:14 specifies that the frog-like unclean spirits "are the spirits of devils [*pneuma* of *daimon*]."
18:2 states that "Babylon the great is fallen, is fallen, and is become the habitation of devils [*daimon*], and the hold of every foul spirit [*akathartos pneuma*]."

Demons are Fallen Angels Subsection: Spirit and Soul

Whilst the terms soul and spirit are often used interchangeably within our common parlance; texts such as Hebrews 4:12 and 1 Thessalonians 5:23 employ both terms.

Of course, both terms are similar as the Hebrew or Greek for soul; *nephesh* (Strong's H5315) and *psuche* (or, *psyche*; Strong's G5590) and the Hebrew or Greek for spirit; *ruach* (Strong's H7307) and *pneuma* (Strong's G4151) all refer to *breath, wind, an air current*, etc.

There are also apparent metaphoric usages of *spirit* as in Colossians 2:5 where Paul writes:

> For though I be absent in the flesh,
> yet am I with you in the spirit, joying
> and beholding your order, and the
> stedfastness of your faith in Christ.

Genesis 2:7 states the following about the creation of Adam, "And the LORD God formed man of the dust of the ground, and breathed into his nostrils the breath of life; and man became a living soul."

God *naphach* (Strong's H5301) into his nostrils the *neshamah* (Strong's H5397, "a puff, that is, wind" blast, breath, etc. *naphach* is the root of *neshamah*) of life; and man became a living *nephesh* (Strong's H5315).

Thus, the *naphach* of God infuses the *neshamah* into Adam which causes him to become a living *nephesh*.

1 Corinthians 15:45 refers to this event as follows, "And so it is written, The first man Adam was made a living soul [*psuche*]; the last Adam was made a quickening spirit [*zoopoieo* (Strong's G2227)]." This last term refers "to (re-) vitalize (literally or figuratively): - make alive, give life, quicken."

Job 27:3 states, "All the while my breath [*neshamah*] is in me, and the spirit [*ruach*] of God is in my nostrils..." and 33:4 states, "The Spirit [*ruach*] of God hath made me, and the breath [*neshamah*] of the Almighty hath given me life."

Demons are *spirits* but are not, or do not seem to have, *souls* and as we saw there are "spirits of devils."

Metaphorically correlating a computer with a human, we may note that a computer is composed of *hardware* into which *software* is installed and yet, none of it functions without *electricity*. The human body is like the hardware, the soul is the software and the spirit is the electricity. Now, the electricity gives the soul the ability to express itself and the body gives it a vehicle through which to express itself.

The initial breath of life into Adam was the electric charge which thereafter, Adam passed on via genetic batteries (continuing with our computer metaphor). The batteries come packaged within the hardware and the animated hardware contains the individual and unique software (the individual soul).

A computer can sustain damage to the point that the hardware breaks and the software can no longer express itself through it. Yet, this does not mean that the software does not or no longer exists but only that it cannot express itself through that particular piece of hardware. At death, the body becomes like the broken computer's hardware.

Keeping in mind that all metaphors eventually break down because they are, after all, just that; metaphorical, note that one could remove the software from the hardware and install it into another computer/hardware so that it may express itself. What happens at death is that the hardware/body is broken, the software/soul goes to be with God and then God creates new resurrected hardware/body into which He installs the software/soul (a 2.0 body).

Revelation 6:9 and 20:4 notes that John "saw under the altar the souls of them that were slain for the word of God....the souls of them that were beheaded for the witness of Jesus, and for the word of God."

In 16:3 an "Angel poured out his vial upon the sea; and it became as the blood of a dead man: and every living soul died in the sea."

18:13 notes that one of the things that was sold as merchandise in Mystery Babylon is "souls of men." *Psyche anthropos* (Strong's G5590 and G444) with *psyche* being breath, vital force, seat of feelings,

desires, affections, aversions, soul, etc. Some versions translate this verse ending as follows:[1]
ASV, KJV & WEB "slaves, and souls of men"
HCSB, NASB & NET "slaves and human lives"
ESV & RSV "slaves, that is, human souls"
DBY, NKJV & YLT "bodies, and souls of men"
HNV "bodies, and people's souls"
NAB "slaves, that is, human beings"
NIV "human beings sold as slaves"
NLT "bodies—that is, human slaves"

The software is thus awaiting new hardware. Romans 6:12 refers to the "mortal body" *thnetos soma* (Strong's G2349 and G4983) and 8:23 to "the redemption of our body."

1 Corinthians 6:20 states "glorify God in your body, and in your spirit, which are God's" and 7:34 "be holy both in body and in spirit." Chapter 15 gets to our context:

> ...since by man came death, by man came also the resurrection of the dead. For as in Adam all die, even so in Christ shall all be made alive. But every man in his own order: Christ the firstfruits; afterward they that are Christ's at his coming...The last enemy that shall be destroyed is death...But some man will say, How are the dead raised up? and with what body do they come?

The text then notes that when a seed is planted that particular organism that would not change unless it was planted dies, as it were, so that it may be made alive and turn into a plant. The same genetic material is thus expressed through very different vehicles; the seed and the plant. The text then continues by noting:

> There are also celestial [epouranios (Strong's G2032)] bodies, and bodies terrestrial [epigeios (Strong's G1919)]: but the glory of the celestial is one, and the glory of the terrestrial is another...So also is the resurrection of the dead.
>
> It is sown in corruption; it is raised in incorruption: It is sown in dishonour; it is raised in glory: it is sown in weakness; it is raised in power: It is sown a natural body [psychikos (Strong's G5591)]; it is raised a spiritual body [pneumatikos (Strong's G4152)].
>
> There is a natural body, and there is a spiritual body.
> And so it is written, The first man Adam was made a living soul; the last Adam was made a quickening spirit. Howbeit that was not first which is spiritual, but that which is natural; and afterward that which is spiritual. The first man is of the Earth, Earthy; the second man is the Lord from heaven...
>
> Behold, I shew you a mystery; We shall not all sleep [symbolic of death], but we shall all be changed, In a moment, in the twinkling of an

eye, at the last trump: for the trumpet
shall sound, and the dead shall be
raised incorruptible, and we shall be
changed.

For this corruptible must put on
incorruption, and this mortal must
put on immortality. So when this
corruptible shall have put on
incorruption, and this mortal shall
have put on immortality, then shall
be brought to pass the saying that is
written, Death is swallowed up in
victory.

2 Corinthians 5:6 states that "whilst we are at home
in the body, we are absent from the Lord" and 5:8
that being "absent from the body" is to "be present
with the Lord."

Philippians 3:21 notes that God will "change our
vile body, that it may be fashioned like unto his
glorious body."

1 Thessalonians 5:23 states, "I pray God your whole
spirit and soul and body be preserved blameless
unto the coming of our Lord Jesus Christ."

James 2:26 plainly states, "the body without the
spirit is dead." John 11:24-25 relates the death of
Jesus' friend Lazarus and that "Martha saith unto
him, I know that he shall rise again in the
resurrection at the last day" but that "Jesus said unto
her, I am the resurrection, and the life: he that
believeth in me, though he were dead, yet shall he
live..." so that she would understand that Lazarus

does not have to wait until the *end times* resurrection, as it were, so that Lazarus rose at Jesus' command.

Matthew 27:52-53 specifies that after Jesus' resurrection "the graves were opened; and many bodies of the saints which slept arose, And came out of the graves after his resurrection, and went into the holy city, and appeared unto many."

1 Thessalonians 4:14-17 notes:
> For if we believe that Jesus died and rose again, even so them also which sleep in Jesus will God bring with him. For this we say unto you by the word of the Lord, that we which are alive and remain unto the coming of the Lord shall not prevent them which are asleep.
>
> For the Lord himself shall descend from heaven with a shout, with the voice of the Archangel, and with the trump of God: and the dead in Christ shall rise first: Then we which are alive and remain shall be caught up together with them in the clouds, to meet the Lord in the air: and so shall we ever be with the Lord.

As an explanatory note; the word *prevent* in the statement "we which are alive...shall not prevent them which are asleep [deceased]" was a way of saying *come before, precede, anticipate,* etc. (*phthano* (Strong's G5348): in short, prevent refers to pre event, before the event.

Recall that Revelation 20:4 referred to "the souls of them that were beheaded for the witness of Jesus." Well, that verse continues by stating that "they lived and reigned with Christ a thousand years."

Following (verses 5-6), we learn that "the rest of the dead lived not again until the thousand years were finished. This is the first resurrection. Blessed and holy is he that hath part in the first resurrection: on such the second death hath no power, but they shall be priests of God and of Christ, and shall reign with him a thousand years."

This is because as per John 5:29 there is a "resurrection of life" and a "resurrection of damnation." As it has been stated: *born twice, die once, born once, die twice*—you must be born again (John 3:3).

Revelation 2:11 specifies that "He that overcometh shall not be hurt of the second death" and 20:14 that "death and hell were cast into the lake of fire. This is the second death" (also see Revelation 21:8).

The basic point seems to be that all *natural terrestrial bodies* will be discarded and will be replaced by *spiritual bodies* (keep in mind that, as noted with the *Shape Shifting Angels?* section of *What Does the Bible Say About Angels?*, *spiritual* body is not the same as what some term the *spirit* body as "spirit body" is a contradiction in terms since "a spirit hath not flesh and bones" (Luke 24:39) but a body does have flesh and bones).

Thus, when Jesus returns to reign on Earth for one thousand years; those who are still alive and those who are deceased will both receive new, resurrected, glorified, spiritual bodies. Thus, for those deceased; their bodies have been entombed (buried in the Earth, at sea, turned to dust and ashes, etc.) but will be quickened just like the seed dies and becomes a plant.

The preceding pages have been leading to the goal of identifying and defining demons and it is to that which we finally come.

The "Angels that sinned," they "which kept not their first estate, but left their own habitation" during the Genesis 6 affair (the *sons of God* Angels) were "delivered…into chains of darkness, to be reserved unto judgment" that is "the judgment of the great day" (see 2 Peter 2:4 and Jude 6).

Consider some of Jesus' interactions with demons: In Matthew 8:29 the *devils* said, "What have we to do with thee, Jesus, thou Son of God? art thou come hither to torment us before the time?" This is paralleled in Mark 5:7 with the *unclean spirit* saying, "What have I to do with thee, Jesus, thou Son of the most high God? I adjure thee by God, that thou torment me not."

Also in Luke 8:28 an *unclean spirit* says "What have I to do with thee, Jesus, thou Son of God most high? I beseech thee, torment me not," in verse 31 this text adds that his name was "Legion: because many devils were entered into him. And they besought him that he would not command them to go out into the deep [*abyssos/abyss* Strong's G12]."

As a side note; this is a perfect example of what was meant by noting that there are many terms for malevolent paranormal beings and that these terms may refer to the same beings in a manner which denotes different ranks, abilities, etc. or they may simply be interchangeable terms.

The very same record of the interaction of Jesus with the Gadarene demoniac has that with which he was possessed as being *devils* and *unclean spirits*. Another example is when the Apostles told Jesus "Lord, even the demons are subject" and Jesus replies "the spirits are subject to you" (Luke 10:17, 20).

1 Timothy 4:1 also references spirits and demons, "The Spirit clearly says that in latter times some will abandon the faith and follow deceiving spirits and things taught by demons."

In Mark 1:24 an *unclean spirit* says, "Let us alone; what have we to do with thee, thou Jesus of Nazareth? art thou come to destroy us? I know thee who thou art, the Holy One of God."

Mark 3:11 has *unclean spirits* saying, "Thou art the Son of God" and in Luke 4:41 *devils* say, "Thou art Christ the Son of God."

In Luke 4:34 *a spirit of an unclean devil* said, "Let us alone; what have we to do with thee, thou Jesus of Nazareth? art thou come to destroy us? I know thee who thou art; the Holy One of God."

In Acts 19:15 an *evil spirit* said, "Jesus I know."

Thus, demons, by any other name, recognize Jesus' person and authority and are terrified of being tormented and/or *destroyed* (a term symbolic of condemnation) "before the time." The fallen Angels in the bottomless-Abyss-pit are awaiting judgment which, in their case, will lead to torment as they are condemned.

The conclusion of this mechanism is that it may be possible to correlate humans and fallen Angels as follows.

Human souls are separated from deceased human bodies and will return to them when they are reconstructed, as it were—glorified, resurrected, etc.

Perhaps, when the Angels were incarcerated in the Abyss it was a simile of human death so that their spirits were left to wander the Earth until such a time as they are due to be released from the Abyss at which time they will re-inhabit their bodies.

This may explain their fear of being condemned before the time as if they were to be commanded to go into the Abyss they would re-inhabit their original bodies and would do nothing but be incarcerated for centuries or millennia.
This may also be why there are no demons mentioned in the Book of Revelation with the exception of 9:20 where *daimonion* (Strong's G1140) is translated *demons* or *devils*.

Demons have inspired idolatry, in part, due to their general modus operandi which is to turn everything and anything which God does inside out, upside down and backwards. "God is spirit" (John 4:24) and so no image could be made of a spirit.

Demons are spirit as well (in the sense of not having flesh and bones; Luke 24:39) but if this theory is accurate then they once inhabited bodies and sought to represent this through idols.

Idols denote that an image of a spirit can be made, or that the idol reflects an unseen being, or a being's presumed form, or that the form represents a being's characteristics. Especially relevant is the concept that the spirit of the being can inhabit the idolatrous image which, in this context, mirrors the demon's desire to inhabit a form.

> What say I then? that the idol is any thing, or that which is offered in sacrifice to idols is any thing? But I say, that the things which the Gentiles sacrifice, they sacrifice to devils, and not to God: and I would not that ye should have fellowship with devils.
>
> Ye cannot drink the cup of the Lord, and the cup of devils: ye cannot be partakers of the Lord's table, and of the table of devils (1 Corinthians 10:19-21).

Beyond that which proceeded, additional support from this may come from the fact that, as Angels, they would know exactly who Jesus is; thus, they recognize His person and authority.

They also do not want to be tormented but want to be left to do that which they do; and what is that? Having been previously embodied, they seek embodiment and thus, seek to possess human bodies.

Thus, demons may be the disembodied *sons of God* fallen Angels who will play an *end times* roll when the pit is opened and the demon/spirits re-inhabit their bodies, fight and lose a heavenly war and will end up judged and condemned.

Note that 2 Peter 2:4 seems to imply that the incarcerated Angels are enchained which would refer to having their physical bodies physically chained. If only their bodies are in Tartarus then there would be no need to chain them up as they are not going anywhere; not, at least, until as per my speculation, the demons/spirits reenter their bodies.

The reason why they are terrified of being exorcised is that they do not want to be sent back into their bodies as that would mean being locked away in Tartarus for whatever amount of time remains until they are released therefrom and also because their release will ultimately lead to their damnation.

Thus, they may be chained in case demons re-enter before the time as in such a case, they would reenter their bodies only to find themselves restrained. If they are incarcerated consciously, body and spirit, then being chained up makes sense and my speculation is unfounded (which may actually have happened to the *Legion* whom Jesus sent into the swine and which drowned as per Matthew 8:30-32, Mark 5:12-13 and Luke 8:32-33).

However, the general term employed within the text is words to the effect of *chains of darkness*. Not something to the likes of dark chains but chains of darkness—whatever that means.
Well, there is range of translations of the key portion of the text which results in no need to conclude that the Angels are physically chained body and spirit and I only brought up this issue so as to cover all potential bases (the following bracketed statements are the notes within the translations). Of course, chains could simply be a reference to incarceration.

ASV "cast them down to hell, and committed them to pits of darkness"
DBY "having cast them down to the deepest pit of gloom has delivered them to chains of darkness"
ESV "cast them into hell [Greek *Tartarus*] and committed them to chains [Some manuscripts *pits*] of gloomy darkness"
HCSB "threw them down into Tartarus [= Gk name for a place of divine punishment in the underworld] and delivered them to be kept in chains [Other mss read *in pits*] of darkness"
HNV "cast them down to Tartarus, and committed them to pits of darkness"
KJV, NKJV "delivered them into chains of darkness"
NAB "condemned them to the chains of Tartarus"
NASB "cast them into hell and committed them to pits of darkness"
NET "threw them into hell and locked them up in chains in utter darkness"

NIV "putting them in chains of darkness [Some manuscripts *in gloomy dungeons*]"
NLT "threw them into hell, [Greek *Tartarus*] in gloomy pits of darkness, [Some manuscripts read *in chains of gloom*]"
RSV "cast them into hell and committed them to pits of nether gloom"
WEB "cast them down to hell, and delivered them into chains of darkness"
YLT "with chains of thick gloom, having cast them down to Tartarus"

Another text to consider within the current context is 1 Peter 3:18-20 which states:
> For Christ also hath once suffered for sins, the just for the unjust, that he might bring us to God, being put to death in the flesh, but quickened by the Spirit:

> By which also he went and preached unto the spirits in prison; Which sometime were disobedient, when once the longsuffering of God waited in the days of Noah, while the ark was a preparing, wherein few, that is, eight souls were saved by water.

Herein *prison* is not specified as a reference to some place such as Tartarus (which it could be even if not specified to be such) but generically to a prison as the term is *phylake* (Strong's G5438 in the KJV as prison (36x), watch (6x), imprisonment (2x), hold (1x), cage (1x), ward (1x)).
Yet, the overall context is clear as it specifies that "the spirits" who are, after all, "in prison"

(apparently the one that is later specified by Peter himself to be Tartarus) "were disobedient...in the days of Noah" which is the very context of the Genesis 6 affair.

But what did He preach? One would imagine that it was His primary message, the gospel of salvation, and yet we have no indication that fallen Angels can, or would, repent. Of course, to preach does not solely refer to the gospel but to heralding a message which may have been that He conquered life and death, has been resurrected and will ascend to take His rightful place of authority.

After all, that very chapter concludes with the following statement about Jesus "Who is gone into heaven, and is on the right hand of God; **angels and authorities and powers being made subject unto him**."

Of course, if *spirits* refers to the fallen Angels then they are physically in prison which is how they could be preached to therein and that would make my speculation unfounded.

Yet, another thing to ponder is whether "the spirits in prison" who "were disobedient...in the days of Noah" refers to human beings and/or the "giants" (and not the Angels) since, after all, the text does refer to the "few" humans that "were saved" in contradistinction.

Another text to consider peradventure some may appeal to it within the current musing is Ephesians 4 which begins with Paul referring to himself thusly, "I therefore, the **prisoner** of the Lord" (that is "bound, in bonds, a captive, a prisoner") following by expressing that he is "Endeavouring to keep the unity of the Spirit in the **bond** of peace" then stating that "unto every one of us is given grace according to the measure of the **gift** of Christ."

Now, he writes that when Jesus "ascended up on high, he **led captivity captive**, and gave **gifts** unto men" and reasons thusly, "Now that he ascended, what is it but that he also descended first into the **lower parts of the earth**? He that descended is the same also that ascended up far above all heavens, that he might fill all things."

Captivity captive is *aichmaloteuo aichmalosia* (Strong's G162 & G161) and *the lower parts of the earth* is *katoteros meros ge* (Strong's G2737, G3313 and G1093).

Without much specificity we are left to speculate and this leads me to ponder whether having "led captivity captive" apparently from "the lower parts of the earth" refers to the location that Luke 19:22 specifies is *Abraham's bosom.*

Luke 19 is the only elucidating text on this location and it refers to "a certain rich man" who "fared sumptuously every day" but appears to have had no regard for those in need such as "a certain beggar named Lazarus." Lazarus was not cared for by the rich man but "laid at his gate, full of sores" and "fed with the crumbs which fell from the rich man's table."

When "the beggar died, and was carried by the angels into Abraham's bosom: the rich man also died, and was buried" and found himself in "hell" which, in this case, is *hades* (Strong's G86) where he was "in torments" and about which he stated "I am tormented in this flame."

He could see "Abraham afar off, and Lazarus in his bosom" and when he requested that Lazarus "may dip the tip of his finger in water, and cool my tongue," Abraham replied, "remember that thou in thy lifetime receivedst thy good things, and likewise Lazarus evil things: but now he is comforted, and thou art tormented." Abraham also specifies that "between us and you there is a great gulf fixed: so that they which would pass from hence to you cannot; neither can they pass to us, that [would come] from thence."

Thus, it appears that before Jesus' salvific atoning act the saved, as it were, went to Abraham's bosom and the unsaved, as it were, to Hades. Thus, the 1 Peter and Ephesians texts may be referring to Jesus, having *preached unto the spirits in prison* and ascending whilst He *led captivity captive* that is, after having *descended first into the lower parts of the earth.*

Another issue to consider is that it appears that, for whatever reason, sometimes demons or spirits are case out of people and are left to roam about and sometimes they are case into the Abyss. Or, it may be that, for whatever reason, only Jesus could cast them into the Abyss while others can only cast them out and they are left to roam about.

For example, "it came to pass, as we went to prayer, a certain damsel possessed with a spirit of divination met us, which brought her masters much gain by soothsaying…Paul, being grieved, turned and said to the spirit, I command thee in the name of Jesus Christ to come out of her. And he came out the same hour" (Acts 16:16, 18). In this case, we are told that the spirit "came out" but what happened to it thereafter is not specified.

Jesus did sometimes specify that He was banishing cast out (exorcized) demons or spirits to the Abyss but He also specified that "When the unclean spirit is gone out of a man, he walketh through dry places, seeking rest, and findeth none. Then he saith, I will return into my house from whence I came out; and when he is come, he findeth it empty, swept, and garnished. Then goeth he, and taketh with himself seven other spirits more wicked than himself, and they enter in and dwell there: and the last state of that man is worse than the first" (Matthew 12:43-45a).

I can only reiterate that this is all very speculative regardless of in which direction one takes it.

Spirits

Hereafter various terms for one or various beings called *spirits* (*pneuma,* Strong's G4151) will be considered.

> Paul, being grieved, turned and said to the spirit, I command thee in the name of Jesus Christ to come out of her (Acts 16:18).

Revelation 16:13 refers to "three unclean spirits like frogs" that "come out of the mouth of the dragon, and out of the mouth of the beast, and out of the mouth of the false prophet" and in verse 14 goes on to specify that "they are the spirits of devils."

Spirit Kinds

Mathew 17 relates that "there came to him [Jesus] a certain man, kneeling down to him, and saying, Lord, have mercy on my son: for he is lunatick, and sore vexed: for ofttimes he falleth into the fire, and oft into the water."

For the sake of clarity, note that the word *lunatick* is being translated as such (and as epileptic in the ESV) from *seleniazomai* (Strong's G4583) "to *be moon struck*, that is, *crazy*: - be lunatic."

The issue that arises is as follows as a conversation ensues between the man and Jesus and later Jesus and the disciples:

> And I brought him to thy disciples,
> and they could not cure him.
> Then Jesus answered and said, O
> faithless and perverse generation,
> how long shall I be with you? how
> long shall I suffer you? bring him
> hither to me. And Jesus rebuked the
> devil; and he departed out of him:
> and the child was cured from that
> very hour.

> Then came the disciples to Jesus
> apart, and said, Why could not we
> cast him out?

> And Jesus said unto them, Because
> of your unbelief: for verily I say unto
> you, If ye have faith as a grain of
> mustard seed, ye shall say unto this

mountain, Remove hence to yonder
place; and it shall remove; and
nothing shall be impossible unto you.
Howbeit this kind goeth not out but
by prayer and fasting.

The NASB excludes this last verse (v. 21) and
directs one's attention to a marginal note stating,
"Some late mss. add verse 21, '*But this kind does
not go our except by prayer and fasting.*'"

A similar occurrence is recorded in Mark 9 as
follows:

And one of the multitude answered
and said, Master, I have brought unto
thee my son, which hath a dumb [as
in mute] spirit; And wheresoever he
taketh him, he teareth him: and he
foameth, and gnasheth with his teeth,
and pineth away: and I spake to thy
disciples that they should cast him
out; and they could not.

He answereth him, and saith, O
faithless generation, how long shall I
be with you? how long shall I suffer
you? bring him unto me. And they
brought him unto him: and when he
saw him, straightway the spirit tare
him; and he fell on the ground, and
wallowed foaming. And he asked his
father, How long is it ago since this
came unto him?

And he said, Of a child [as in, from
childhood]. And ofttimes it hath cast

him into the fire, and into the waters,
to destroy him: but if thou canst do
any thing, have compassion on us,
and help us.

Jesus said unto him, If thou canst
believe, all things are possible to him
that believeth.
And straightway the father of the
child cried out, and said with tears,
Lord, I believe; help thou mine
unbelief.

When Jesus saw that the people
came running together, he rebuked
the foul spirit, saying unto him, Thou
dumb and deaf spirit, I charge thee,
come out of him, and enter no more
into him. And the spirit cried, and
rent him sore, and came out of him:
and he was as one dead; insomuch
that many said, He is dead. But Jesus
took him by the hand, and lifted him
up; and he arose.

And when he was come into the
house, his disciples asked him
privately, Why could not we cast
him out? And he said unto them,
This kind can come forth by nothing,
but by prayer and fasting.

The NASB excludes the terms "and fasting" from
the last verse (v. 29) and notes "Many mss. add: *and
fasting*" (note that such a circumstance is also
related in Luke 9:38-42 and yet, in a succinct

enough manner that there is no further record of the discussion after the exorcism).

Thus, in the first instance, Jesus may or may not have noted that there are different kinds of demons and in the second, He either stated that those of "this kind" come out by *prayer* alone or by *prayer and fasting.*
The point for our purposes is that there are different kinds as per Mark (and, as we shall see, Matthew 12 and Luke 11) although how they differ is unstated.

Are they ontologically different (in nature and essence)? There is no indication that there are different kinds of beings who are, nevertheless, all designated as *spirits* (in the demonic sense of malicious possession).

Are they of different strength and/or authority? It could very well be as Matthew 12:43-45 (reiterated in Luke 11:24-26) note that "When the unclean spirit is gone out of a man" but comes back to find the "house" the body which he left, "empty" as in without God inhabiting it and also "swept, and garnished" as in temporarily cleaned up, the spirit comes back with "seven other spirits <u>more wicked than himself.</u>"

Are they different due to circumstances? This is, indeed, an issue that is distinguished by demonologists, exorcists and deliverance ministers as denoting the difference between being demonically influenced or demonically possessed.

For example, someone who is living the lifestyle of a garden variety sinner, as it were, could be demonically influenced. On the other hand, someone who fashions themselves a medium, channeler, psychic, or some such thing, opens themselves up for demons to enter them.

That is, presumably they give legal permission for possession even if they do not consider it as such (such as in the case of being to whom someone may refer as *ascended masters*, *higher beings*, etc.).

Note that the Bible does not seem to indicate that a function of demons is to cause humans to sin. Rather, there is "another law in my members, warring against the law of my mind, and bringing me into captivity to the law of sin which is in my members" (Romans 7:23), "every man is tempted, when he is drawn away of his own lust, and enticed. Then when lust hath conceived, it bringeth forth sin: and sin, when it is finished, bringeth forth death" (James 1:14-15) and "wars and fightings" come "among you...even of your lusts that war in your members" since "Ye lust, and have not: ye kill, and desire to have, and cannot obtain: ye fight and war, yet ye have not, because ye ask not" (James 4:1-2).

Shedim

The term *shed* (Strong's H7700) is "a *daemon* (as *malignant*): - devil." It comes from *shud* (Strong's H7736) which is a primitive root, "properly to *swell* up, that is, figuratively (by implication of *insolence*) to *devastate*: - waste."

Gesenius' Hebrew-Chaldee Lexicon note that this word is only found in the plural, thus *shedim*, and refers to idols as the root denotes to rule whence lord, master and in Syriac *demon*. The Latin Vulgate translates as *dæmonia*, "since the Jews [rightly] regarded idols to be demons, who allowed themselves to be worshipped by men" (brackets in original).

The term *shedim* appears twice, as follows, wherein it is translated as *devils*:
>They sacrificed unto devils, not to God; to gods whom they knew not, to new gods that came newly up, whom your fathers feared not (Deuteronomy 32:17).

>Yea, they sacrificed their sons and their daughters unto devils... (Psalm 106:37).

Satyr

The word *sa'iyr* (Strong's H8163) refers to "shaggy; as noun, a he goat; by analogy a faun: - devil, goat, hairy, kid, rough, satyr." Its primitive root is *sa'ar* (Strong's H8175), "to storm; by implication to *shiver*, that is, *fear*: - be (horribly) afraid, fear, hurl as a storm, be tempestuous, come like (take away as with) a whirlwind."

Strong's notes that "satyr, may refer to a demon possessed goat like the swine of Gadara (Mt. 8:30-32)" with Gadara referring to the country of the *Gergesenes/Gadarenes*.

A demon possessed goat, really? Demon possessed animals do not appear in the biblical texts with, that is, one possible exception; the aforementioned "swine of Gadara" (do not worry, I will not make the joke about deviled ham—oops, guess I did).

The issue is that the context is not of demons routinely seeking animals for possession. If that was the case then they surely would do so routinely. The case of the swine is one in which the demons are afraid to be cast into the *abyssos/abyss* (Strong's G12 translated as "the deep" in the KJV) and asking Jesus to allow them to enter the swine:

> So the devils besought him, saying, If thou cast us out, suffer us to go away into the herd of swine. And he said unto them, Go. And when they were come out, they went into the herd of swine... (Matthew 8:31-32)

> And all the devils besought him,
> saying, Send us into the swine, that
> we may enter into them. And
> forthwith Jesus gave them leave.
> And the unclean spirits went out, and
> entered into the swine... (Mark 5:12-
> 13)

> And there was there an herd of many
> swine feeding on the mountain: and
> they besought him that he would
> suffer them to enter into them. And
> he suffered them. Then went the
> devils out of the man, and entered
> into the swine... (Luke 8:32-33)

This appears to be a very special circumstance.
Incidentally, within these texts *devils* is the Greek
daimon.

Yet, in any regard *sa'iyr* is a word with many
meanings and/or one that is used in a variety of
ways:

> And Jacob said to Rebekah his
> mother, Behold, Esau my brother is a
> hairy [sa'iyr] man, and I am a smooth
> man... (Genesis 27:11).

> And they shall no more offer their
> sacrifices unto devils [sa'iyr], after
> whom they have gone a whoring.
> This shall be a statute for ever unto
> them throughout their generations
> (Leviticus 17:7, compare to
> Deuteronomy 32:17 above).

> And he ordained him priests for the
> high places, and for the devils
> [sa'iyr], and for the calves which he
> had made (2 Chronicles 11:15).

> But wild beasts of the desert shall lie
> there; and their houses shall be full
> of doleful creatures; and owls shall
> dwell there, and satyrs [sa'iyr] shall
> dance there (Isaiah 13:21).

> The wild beasts of the desert shall
> also meet with the wild beasts of the
> island, and the satyr [sa'iyr] shall cry
> to his fellow; the screech owl also
> shall rest there, and find for herself a
> place of rest (Isaiah 34:14).

Mythically satyrs are generally depicted as half
human and half goats (consider Pan for example).
However, there is no reason to read such a meaning
into the text of Leviticus or Isaiah since that would
be against grammatical context, historical context
and cultural context.

We should never take a text out of context to make
a pretext for a proof-text.
As is the case with unicorns (which will be
considered within their own section) the Bible
employs the term *sa'iyr* but never describes half
humans and half goats.

As we have seen, *sa'iyr* seems to primarily refer to
being hairy such as with the mere human Esau and
is thus, a term that is applied to hairy/furry animals.
For that matter, there are two words for *hairy* which

are clearly related and both are used of Esau. Genesis 27:11 has him being "a hairy [sa'iyr] man" while Genesis 25:25 had him being "like an hairy [*se'ar* or *sa'ar*] garment."

The context of the 2 Chronicles text is devils and calves which, since one animal is clearly referred to, likely contextually means that the *devils* are simply some hairy/furry animal.

The Leviticus text is more in keeping with this chapter's context of being about demons. However, there is no real description therein but that they sacrifices unto sa'iyr; perhaps it was an idol depicting a goat (shaggy goat), goat-like, or otherwise hairy/furry animal.

Likewise with the two Isaiah texts as "wild beasts...doleful ["a *howler* or lonesome wild animal"] creatures....screech owl" where the *sa'iyr* appears, again, to simply be a hairy/furry animal.

"Assyrian Goat Demons. Carvings
on a boulder. After Lenormant"
From Paul Carus, *The History of the Devil
and the Idea of Evil from the Earliest
Times to the Present Day* (1900 AD)

For a comparison to the Isaiah texts above, note
Jeremiah 50:39 "...the wild beasts of the desert with
the wild beasts of the islands shall dwell there, and
the owls shall dwell therein: and it shall be no more
inhabited for ever; neither shall it be dwelt in from
generation to generation."

This was a manner whereby to refer to desolate
former dwelling places such as cities. Herein we
saw no reference to mythical goat-men or even to
hairy/furry animals for that matter.

Within a different historical, cultural and
grammatical context we find Revelation 18:2

stating, "…Babylon the great is fallen, is fallen, and is become the habitation of devils [*daimon*], and the hold of every foul spirit [*akathartos pneuma*], and a cage of every unclean and hateful bird [*akathartos kai miseo orneon*]." Yet, still no mythological creatures.

Evil Spirits

This term is also relevant to our consideration of *demons* along with which came a consideration of *devils*. This term consists of *ra' ruwach* (Strong's H7451 and H7307) the definition of which is simply straightforward and rightly translated as *evil* and *spirit*.

The fascinating thing about evil spirits is that what is being referred to are not, generically, any and all demons, devils, Satan, etc. but the terminology is very specific and seems to imply that it is a spirit that is sent by God to commit an evil act. While God did not build, as it were, evil into His original creation He appears to be shown employing it towards His ultimate and sovereign ends.

For example, God states, "I form the light, and create darkness: I make peace, and create evil: I the LORD do all these things" (Isaiah 45:7). Of course, the context is not the original creation but that which occurs thereafter, that which God does with His creation even after its fall. In fact, the context itself makes it clear that the original creative event is not envisaged.

The verse is referring to opposites the first of which is light versus dark and the second one which is peace versus—well, actually evil is not the opposite of peace. Now, the word which is opposite of peace, the one translated as *evil* in the KJV is *ra'/ra'ah* which refers to adversity, affliction, bad, calamity, displeasure, distress, evil, etc. Thus, within contexts such as this one it is rendered *calamity* (as the

NASB and NKJV have for this text), *disaster* (in the NIV) and *woe* (in the NAB and RSV). These terms better fit the context as they are opposites of peace (the JPS has *evil*).

Moreover, when God employs evil/calamity/disaster it is towards a redemptive end as Joseph puts it when his brothers, who had sold him, are afraid that he, who then gained great authority and power, would retaliate against them, "But as for you, ye thought evil against me; but God meant it unto good, to bring to pass, as it is this day, to save much people alive" (Genesis 50:20).

The texts in which the term *evil spirit* specifically appears is as follows and accounts for the work of two authors; the authors of Judges and Samuel:

> Then God sent an evil spirit between Abimelech and the men of Shechem... (Judges 9:23).

> But the Spirit of the LORD departed from Saul, and an evil spirit from the LORD troubled him. And Saul's servants said unto him, Behold now, an evil spirit from God troubleth thee.

> Let our lord now command thy servants, which are before thee, to seek out a man, who is a cunning player on an harp: and it shall come to pass, when the evil spirit from God is upon thee, that he shall play with his hand, and thou shalt be well...

And it came to pass, when the evil
spirit from God was upon Saul, that
David took an harp, and played with
his hand: so Saul was refreshed, and
was well, and the evil spirit departed
from him (1 Samuel 16:14-16, 23).

And it came to pass on the morrow,
that the evil spirit from God came
upon Saul... (1 Samuel 18:10).

And the evil spirit from the LORD
was upon Saul (1 Samuel 19:9).

In the New Testament we find the term as *poneros
pneuma* (Strong's G4190 and G4151) which, again,
is straightforward and appears solely within the text
of Acts 19:15-16 wherein self-styled exorcists, who
were not following Jesus:

...took upon them to call over them
which had evil spirits the name of
the Lord Jesus, saying, We adjure
you by Jesus whom Paul preacheth.
And there were seven sons of one
Sceva, a Jew, and chief of the priests,
which did so.

And the evil spirit answered and
said, Jesus I know, and Paul I know;
but who are ye? And the man in
whom the evil spirit was leaped on
them, and overcame them, and
prevailed against them, so that they
fled out of that house naked and
wounded.

Lying Spirits

In this case, we are dealing with deception as *sheqer ruach* (Strong's H8267) refers to "an untruth; by implication a sham (often adverbially): - without a cause, deceit (-ful), false (-hood, -ly), feignedly, liar, + lie, lying, vain (thing), wrongfully."

We find a specific reference to a *lying spirit* in the following text of 1 Kings 22 pertaining to the prophet Micaiah:

...I saw the LORD sitting on his throne, and all the host of heaven standing by him on his right hand and on his left. And the LORD said, Who shall persuade Ahab, that he may go up and fall at Ramothgilead? And one said on this manner, and another said on that manner.

And there came forth a spirit, and stood before the LORD, and said, I will persuade him. And the LORD said unto him, Wherewith? And he said, I will go forth, and I will be a lying spirit in the mouth of all his prophets. And he said, Thou shalt persuade him, and prevail also: go forth, and do so.

Now therefore, behold, the LORD hath put a lying spirit in the mouth of all these thy prophets, and the LORD hath spoken evil concerning thee.

This is reiterated in 2 Chronicles 18:21-22 as follows:

> And he said, I will go out, and be a lying spirit in the mouth of all his prophets. And the LORD said, Thou shalt entice him, and thou shalt also prevail: go out, and do even so. Now therefore, behold, the LORD hath put a lying spirit in the mouth of these thy prophets, and the LORD hath spoken evil against thee.

As noted in the previous section; God does not ontologically create but does employ evil/calamity/disaster.

Unclean Spirits

Just as with *evil* and *lying spirit*, the words of which *unclean spirit* consists are very straightforward; the Hebrew is *ṭum'ah ruach* (Strong's H2932 and H7307) and in Greek *akathartos pneuma* (Strong's G169 and G4151).

It appears in one Old Testament text and a few New Testament texts:

> ...saith the LORD of hosts...I will cause the prophets and the unclean spirit to pass out of the land (Zechariah 13:2).

> ...the unclean spirit is gone out of a man... (Matthew 12:43).

> ...a man with an unclean spirit...the unclean spirit had torn him, and cried with a loud voice, he came out of him (Mark 1:23, 26).

> ...they said, He hath an unclean spirit (Mark 3:30).

> ...there met him out of the tombs a man with an unclean spirit....[Jesus] said unto him, Come out of the man, thou unclean spirit (Mark 5:2, 8).

> For a certain woman, whose young daughter had an unclean spirit, heard of him, and came and fell at his feet (Mark 7:25).

...he had commanded the unclean
spirit to come out of the man...
(Luke 8:29).

...Jesus rebuked the unclean spirit,
and healed the child, and delivered
him again to his father (Luke 9:42).

...the unclean spirit is gone out of a
man... (Luke 11:24).

Additionally, the following have
some descriptive value with regards
to unclean spirits.

...how can one enter into a strong
man's house, and spoil his goods,
except he first bind the strong man?
and then he will spoil his house
(Matthew 12:29).

No man can enter into a strong man's
house, and spoil his goods, except he
will first bind the strong man; and
then he will spoil his house (Mark
3:27-29).

When the unclean spirit is gone out
of a man, he walketh through dry
places, seeking rest, and findeth
none. Then he saith, I will return into
my house from whence I came out;
and when he is come, he findeth it
empty, swept, and garnished.

Then goeth he, and taketh with himself seven other spirits more wicked than himself, and they enter in and dwell there: and the last state of that man is worse than the first. Even so shall it be also unto this wicked generation (Matthew 12:43-45 reiterated in Luke 11:24-26).

Daimonion

Daimonion (Strong's G1140) is generally translated as *devils*. It is a neuter of a derivative of *daimon* and refers to "a *daemonic being*; by extension a *deity*: - devil, god."

> Many will say to me in that day,
> Lord, Lord, have we not prophesied
> in thy name? and in thy name have
> cast out devils? and in thy name
> done many wonderful works?
> (Matthew 7:22).

> And when the devil was cast out, the
> dumb spake: and the multitudes
> marvelled, saying, It was never so
> seen in Israel. But the Pharisees said,
> He casteth out devils through the
> prince of the devils (Matthew 9:33-
> 34).

> Heal the sick, cleanse the lepers,
> raise the dead, cast out devils: freely
> ye have received, freely give
> (Matthew 10:8).

> For John came neither eating nor
> drinking, and they say, He hath a
> devil (Matthew 11:18).
> For John the Baptist came neither
> eating bread nor drinking wine; and
> ye say, He hath a devil (Luke 7:33).

But when the Pharisees heard it, they said, This fellow doth not cast out devils, but by Beelzebub the prince of the devils.
And if I by Beelzebub cast out devils, by whom do your children cast them out? therefore they shall be your judges.
But if I cast out devils by the Spirit of God, then the kingdom of God is come unto you (Matthew 12:24, 27-28).

And Jesus rebuked the devil; and he departed out of him: and the child was cured from that very hour (Matthew 17:18).

And he healed many that were sick of divers diseases, and cast out many devils; and suffered not the devils to speak, because they knew him. And he preached in their synagogues throughout all Galilee, and cast out devils (Mark 1:34, 39).

And to have power to heal sicknesses, and to cast out devils: And the scribes which came down from Jerusalem said, He hath Beelzebub, and by the prince of the devils casteth he out devils (Mark 3:15, 22).

And they cast out many devils, and
anointed with oil many that were
sick, and healed them (Mark 6:13).

The woman was a Greek, a
Syrophenician by nation; and she
besought him that he would cast
forth the devil out of her daughter.
And he said unto her, For this saying
go thy way; the devil is gone out of
thy daughter. And when she was
come to her house, she found the
devil gone out, and her daughter laid
upon the bed (Mark 7:26, 29-30).

And John answered him, saying,
Master, we saw one casting out
devils in thy name, and he followeth
not us: and we forbad him, because
he followeth not us. But Jesus said,
Forbid him not: for there is no man
which shall do a miracle in my name,
that can lightly speak evil of me. For
he that is not against us is on our part
(Mark 9:38-40).

And John answered and said, Master,
we saw one casting out devils in thy
name; and we forbad him, because
he followeth not with us. And Jesus
said unto him, Forbid him not: for he
that is not against us is for us (Luke
9:49-50).

Now when Jesus was risen early the
first day of the week, he appeared

first to Mary Magdalene, out of
whom he had cast seven devils. And
these signs shall follow them that
believe; In my name shall they cast
out devils; they shall speak with new
tongues… (Mark 16:9, 17).
And certain women, which had been
healed of evil spirits and infirmities,
May called Magdalene, out of whom
went seven devils… (Luke 8:2).

And in the synagogue there was a
man, which had a spirit of an unclean
devil, and cried out with a loud
voice…And Jesus rebuked him,
saying, Hold thy peace, and come
out of him. And when the devil had
thrown him in the midst, he came out
of him, and hurt him not (Luke 4:33,
35).

And devils also came out of many,
crying out, and saying, Thou art
Christ the Son of God. And he
rebuking them suffered them not to
speak: for they knew that he was
Christ (Luke 4:41).

Then he called his twelve disciples
together, and gave them power and
authority over all devils, and to cure
diseases (Luke 9:1).

And the seventy returned again with
joy, saying, Lord, even the devils are

subject unto us through thy name
(Luke 10:17).

And he was casting out a devil, and
it was dumb. And it came to pass,
when the devil was gone out, the
dumb spake; and the people
wondered (Luke 11:14).

And he said unto them, Go ye, and
tell that fox [Herod], Behold, I cast
out devils, and I do cures to day and
to morrow, and the third day I shall
be perfected (Luke 13:32).

Did not Moses give you the law, and
yet none of you keepeth the law?
Why go ye about to kill me? The
people answered and said, Thou hast
a devil: who goeth about to kill thee?
(John 7:19-20).

Then answered the Jews, and said
unto him, Say we not well that thou
art a Samaritan, and hast a devil?
Jesus answered, I have not a devil;
but I honour my Father, and ye do
dishonour me.
Then said the Jews unto him, Now
we know that thou hast a devil.
Abraham is dead, and the prophets;
and thou sayest, If a man keep my
saying, he shall never taste of death
(John 8:48-49, 52).

> And many of them said, He hath a
> devil, and is mad; why hear ye him?
> Others said, These are not the words
> of him that hath a devil. Can a devil
> open the eyes of the blind? (John
> 10:20-21).

> Then certain philosophers of the
> Epicureans, and of the Stoicks,
> encountered him. And some said,
> What will this babbler say? other
> some, He seemeth to be a setter forth
> of strange gods: because he preached
> unto them Jesus, and the resurrection
> (Acts 17:18).

FYI: Epicureans and Stoicks refers to schools of philosophy. *Epikoureios* (Strong's G1946) from *Epikouros* "(compare G1947; a noted philosopher); an Epicurean or follower of Epicurus: - Epicurean." *Stoikos* (Strong's G4770) from G4745 "a stoic" (as occupying a particular porch in Athens), that is, adherent of a certain philosophy: - Stoick."

Devils can cause ailments (although all ailments are not said to be cause by devils) such as muteness and casting them out in Jesus' name/authority brings healing restoration of health, they recognize Jesus and His authority, etc.

> But I say, that the things which the
> Gentiles sacrifice, they sacrifice to
> devils, and not to God: and I would
> not that ye should have fellowship
> with devils. Ye cannot drink the cup
> of the Lord, and the cup of devils: ye

cannot be partakers of the Lord's table, and of the table of devils (1 Corinthians 10:20-21).

Now the Spirit speaketh expressly, that in the latter times some shall depart from the faith, giving heed to seducing spirits, and doctrines of devils; Speaking lies in hypocrisy; having their conscience seared with a hot iron; Forbidding to marry, and commanding to abstain from meats, which God hath created to be received with thanksgiving of them which believe and know the truth (1 Timothy 4:1-3).

Thou believest that there is one God; thou doest well: the devils also believe, and tremble (James 2:19).

And the rest of the men which were not killed by these plagues yet repented not of the works of their hands, that they should not worship devils, and idols of gold, and silver, and brass, and stone, and of wood: which neither can see, nor hear, nor walk... (Revelation 9:20).

Daimon

A related word to *damonion* is *daimon* (Strong's G1142) which comes from a term referring to "*distribute* fortunes" and is more specifically defined as "a *demon* or super natural spirit (of a bad nature): - devil."

The term is found in Matthew 8:31 which is paralleled in Mark 5:12 and also referenced in Luke 8:29. As those texts will be considered in the next section, note the only other two texts in which it occurs:

> For they are the spirits of devils, working miracles, which go forth unto the kings of the Earth and of the whole world, to gather them to the battle of that great day of God Almighty (Revelation 16:14).

> And he cried mightily with a strong voice, saying, Babylon the great is fallen, is fallen, and is become the habitation of devils, and the hold of every foul spirit, and a cage of every unclean and hateful bird (Revelation 18:2).

Gadarene Demoniac

An event recorded by three of the Gospels is that which is generally known as the *Gadarene Demoniac* in reference to the region of Gadara the citizens of which were known as *Gadarenes* or *Gergesenes*.

Matthew references two men and Mark and Luke reference one. Clearly, two men were encountered by Jesus and Mark and Luke chose to focus on one of them.
In fact, while Matthew mentions two men it is clearly in passing as he likewise focuses upon one.
Why one and not the other or one and not both?
There is no telling but speculation concludes that it was the one man whose interaction with Jesus was more telling and therefore more worth retelling.

Matthew 8 has the record as follows:
> And when he was come to the other side into the country of the Gergesenes, there met him two possessed with devils, coming out of the tombs, exceeding fierce, so that no man might pass by that way. And, behold, they cried out, saying, What have we to do with thee, Jesus, thou Son of God? art thou come hither to torment us before the time?
>
> And there was a good way off from them an herd of many swine feeding. So the devils besought him, saying,

If thou cast us out, suffer us to go
away into the herd of swine.
And he said unto them, Go. And
when they were come out, they went
into the herd of swine: and, behold,
the whole herd of swine ran violently
down a steep place into the sea, and
perished in the waters.

And they that kept them fled, and
went their ways into the city, and
told every thing, and what was
befallen to the possessed of the
devils. And, behold, the whole city
came out to meet Jesus: and when
they saw him, they besought him that
he would depart out of their coasts.

Mark 5 has it as follows:
And they came over unto the other
side of the sea, into the country of
the Gadarenes. And when he was
come out of the ship, immediately
there met him out of the tombs a man
with an unclean spirit, Who had his
dwelling among the tombs; and no
man could bind him, no, not with
chains: Because that he had been
often bound with fetters and chains,
and the chains had been plucked
asunder by him, and the fetters
broken in pieces: neither could any
man tame him.

And always, night and day, he was in
the mountains, and in the tombs,

crying, and cutting himself with stones. But when he saw Jesus afar off, he ran and worshipped him, And cried with a loud voice, and said, What have I to do with thee, Jesus, thou Son of the most high God? I adjure thee by God, that thou torment me not. For he said unto him, Come out of the man, thou unclean spirit.

And he asked him, What is thy name? And he answered, saying, My name is Legion: for we are many. And he besought him much that he would not send them away out of the country.

Now there was there nigh unto the mountains a great herd of swine feeding. And all the devils besought him, saying, Send us into the swine, that we may enter into them.

And forthwith Jesus gave them leave. And the unclean spirits went out, and entered into the swine: and the herd ran violently down a steep place into the sea, (they were about two thousand;) and were choked in the sea.

Luke 8 relates it this way:
And when he went forth to land, there met him out of the city a certain man, which had devils long

time, and ware no clothes, neither
abode in any house, but in the tombs.
When he saw Jesus, he cried out, and
fell down before him, and with a
loud voice said, What have I to do
with thee, Jesus, thou Son of God
most high? I beseech thee, torment
me not.

(For he had commanded the unclean
spirit to come out of the man. For
oftentimes it had caught him: and he
was kept bound with chains and in
fetters; and he brake the bands, and
was driven of the devil into the
wilderness.)

And Jesus asked him, saying, What
is thy name? And he said, Legion:
because many devils were entered
into him. And they besought him that
he would not command them to go
out into the deep. And there was
there an herd of many swine feeding
on the mountain: and they besought
him that he would suffer them to
enter into them. And he suffered
them.

Then went the devils out of the man,
and entered into the swine: and the
herd ran violently down a steep place
into the lake, and were choked.
When they that fed them saw what
was done, they fled, and went and
told it in the city and in the country.

Then they went out to see what was
done; and came to Jesus, and found
the man, out of whom the devils
were departed, sitting at the feet of
Jesus, clothed, and in his right mind:
and they were afraid.

They also which saw it told them by
what means he that was possessed of
the devils was healed. Then the
whole multitude of the country of the
Gadarenes round about besought him
to depart from them; for they were
taken with great fear: and he went up
into the ship, and returned back
again.

Now the man out of whom the devils
were departed besought him that he
might be with him: but Jesus sent
him away, saying, Return to thine
own house, and shew how great
things God hath done unto thee. And
he went his way, and published
throughout the whole city how great
things Jesus had done unto him.

These texts are instructive on various points. For the
purposes of the consideration of various terms for
maliciously malevolent beings, note that various
terms are interchangeable. Matthew succinctly
refers to devils. Mark refers to devils and unclean
spirits. Luke refers to devils, the devil and unclean
spirit.

This goes to show that, as noted within the *Angelic and Demonic Ranks* section of *What Does the Bible Say About Angels?*, while there are ranks of maliciously malevolent beings there do not appear to be different kinds.

In short, while *Angels*, *Cherubim*, *Seraphim* and *Ophanim* are different categories of being, *devils* and *unclean spirits* are not (likewise for *evil spirits*, et al.).

Familiar Spirits

Let us begin this section on spirits, in this case *familiar spirits*, with a very telling quote: *Behold, my belly is as wine which hath no vent; it is ready to burst like new bottles* (Job 32:19).

Did you note the reference to *familiar spirits* within this quotation? Well, it is the word *bottles* and appears to have been translated as such due to the fact that the Hebrew term is very elastic due to its metaphorical nature.

The term *'ob* (Strong's H178) comes "From the same as H1 (apparently through the idea of *prattling* a father's name); properly a *mumble*, that is, a water *skin* (from its hollow sound); hence a *necromancer* (ventriloquist, as from a jar): - bottle, familiar spirit." Thus, the Job text is translated as bottles because *water skin* is in reference to a receptacle for holding water (could be a cow or sheep bladder, etc.).

As always, ultimately context, and not etymology, determines meaning. Yet, note that the word *'ob* is said to come from the same as Strong's H1 which is *'ab* which is used for *father* and whence came the more commonly known word *abba* such as in Mark 14:36 when Jesus said, "Abba, Father, all things are possible unto thee" wherein *abba* and *father* are *abba* and *pater* (Strong's G5 and G3962).

As the definition notes, the term *'ob* apparently came to be through the idea of *prattling*, that is childish baby talking, a father's name and thus, a *mumble*, as in to say something quietly and indistinctly. In fact, below you will note that Isaiah 8:19 refers to *wizards that peep, and that mutter*. Isaiah 29:4 seems to focus upon this as follows:

> And thou shalt be brought down, and
> shalt speak out of the ground, and
> thy speech shall be low out of the
> dust, and thy voice shall be, as of one
> that hath a familiar spirit, out of the
> ground, and thy speech shall whisper
> out of the dust.

The reference to a skin used for liquid containment comes in to play as such a skin makes a hollow sound and was related to a *necromancer* in relation to ventriloquism as in having a voice amplified, or so the sense seems to be, via a jar, or bottle (think of blowing into the top of a bottle so as to make a sound). Although, note that the actual term *necromancer* is a composite of *darash* and *muwth* (Strong's H1875 and H4191) referring to seeking the dead.

> Regard not them that have familiar
> spirits, neither seek after wizards, to
> be defiled by them: I am the LORD
> your God (Leviticus 19:31).

> And the soul that turneth after such
> as have familiar spirits, and after
> wizards, to go a whoring after them,
> I will even set my face against that
> soul, and will cut him off from
> among his people. A man also or
> woman that hath a familiar spirit, or
> that is a wizard, shall surely be put to

death: they shall stone them with stones: their blood shall be upon them (Leviticus 20:6).

When thou art come into the land which the LORD thy God giveth thee, thou shalt not learn to do after the abominations of those nations. There shall not be found among you any one that maketh his son or his daughter to pass through the fire, or that useth divination, or an observer of times, or an enchanter, or a witch, Or a charmer, or a consulter with familiar spirits, or a wizard, or a necromancer (Deuteronomy 18:9-11).

And he made his son pass through the fire, and observed times, and used enchantments, and dealt with familiar spirits and wizards: he wrought much wickedness in the sight of the LORD, to provoke him to anger (2 Kings 21:6).

Moreover the workers with familiar spirits, and the wizards, and the images, and the idols, and all the abominations that were spied in the land of Judah and in Jerusalem, did Josiah put away, that he might perform the words of the law which were written in the book that Hilkiah the priest found in the house of the LORD (2 Kings 23:24).

And he caused his children to pass through the fire in the valley of the son of Hinnom: also he observed times, and used enchantments, and used witchcraft, and dealt with a familiar spirit, and with wizards: he wrought much evil in the sight of the LORD, to provoke him to anger (2 Chronicles 33:6).

And when they shall say unto you, Seek unto them that have familiar spirits, and unto wizards that peep, and that mutter: should not a people seek unto their God? for the living to the dead? (Isaiah 8:19).

And the spirit of Egypt shall fail in the midst thereof; and I will destroy the counsel thereof: and they shall seek to the idols, and to the charmers, and to them that have familiar spirits, and to the wizards (Isaiah 19:3).

And thou shalt be brought down, and shalt speak out of the ground, and thy speech shall be low out of the dust, and thy voice shall be, as of one that hath a familiar spirit, out of the ground, and thy speech shall whisper out of the dust (Isaiah 29:4).

One of the most well-known Old Testament tales regarding such issues pertains to King Saul:

...Samuel was dead...And Saul had
put away those that had familiar
spirits, and the wizards, out of the
land...Then said Saul unto his
servants, Seek me a woman that hath
a familiar spirit, that I may go to her,
and enquire of her.

And his servants said to him, Behold,
there is a woman that hath a familiar
spirit at Endor. And Saul disguised
himself, and...came to the woman by
night: and he said...Bring me up
Samuel.

And when the woman saw Samuel,
she cried with a loud voice...And the
king said unto her...what sawest
thou? And the woman said unto
Saul, I saw gods ascending out of the
Earth. And he said unto her, What
form is he of? And she said, An old
man cometh up; and he is covered
with a mantle.

And Saul perceived that it was
Samuel, and he stooped with his face
to the ground, and bowed himself.
And Samuel said to Saul, Why hast
thou disquieted me, to bring me up?
(1 Samuel 28).

Thereafter, a discussion ensues about events
occurring within Israel. Another text that touches
upon this notes:

> So Saul died for his transgression
> which he committed against the
> LORD, even against the word of the
> LORD, which he kept not, and also
> for asking counsel of one that had a
> familiar spirit, to enquire of it... (1
> Chronicles 10:13).

Saul wanted the spirit of Samuel to be raised and found she who is known popularly as the *witch* of Endor who had a familiar spirit. For some reason, about which much has been speculated, when the woman saw Samuel she cried with a loud voice. At this point, she can see something or someone that Saul cannot. She saw gods (*'elohim*) ascending out of the Earth.

The plural term *'elohim* could actually refer to a single individual based on the context. The only one she sees, or the only one she describes, is identified via the description as being Samuel. The conversation ensues either directly (meaning that Saul can hear Samuel) or else with the woman as in intermediary (if she is the only one who could both see and hear Samuel).

Note that Samuel states that being called onto the realm of the living, as it were, is considered to be disquieting as in having disturbed him.

Thus, *familiar spirits* are referred to as beings that someone can *have* and/or otherwise beings with which one can consult; denoting contact and the exchange of information.
Such personages are correlated with *wizards, enchanters, witches, charmers, diviners, observers*

of times and those who *maketh his son or his daughter to pass through the fire* meaning human child sacrifices. It also correlates to idolatrous images and are said to be the cause of defilement, wickedness and amounts to abomination.

Historically, common conceptions of what is generally termed *familiar spirits* is twofold. On the occult side of things they are seen as companions of witches often taking the form of a pet such as a cat.

On the Judeo-Christian worldview theology side they are one or more demons who are *familiar* with a family. That is to say that they hang around, as it were, with family groups perhaps for centuries.

It is unknown whether one or more are assigned per family or one or more are assigned per region, etc. For example, family members may move to other states, countries, etc. and another demon(s) may take over.
Or perhaps, demons can somehow track family groups as we are unaware of just how they interact with us, particularly at that presumed level.

If we have *guardian Angels* perhaps we have *menacing Demons.*

Meet the Idols

1 Corinthians 8 provides a succinct statement regarding idols and the various *gods* whom they represent:

> ...we know that an idol is nothing in
> the world, and that there is none
> other God but one. For though there
> be that are called gods, whether in
> heaven or in earth, (as there be gods
> many, and lords many,)
> But to us there is but one God, the
> Father, of whom are all things, and
> we in him; and one Lord Jesus
> Christ, by whom are all things, and
> we by him.

Thus, there are so called gods, as we would term it, and there are many such gods and lords and yet, only one true God. Hereinafter, I will review some of the idolatrous deities mentioned in the Bible namely Amon, Astaroth, Baal, Lord of the Flies, Belial, Chiun/Remphan, Chemosh, Dagon, Marduk, Molech, Milcom, Nergal, Ashima, Nibhaz Tartak, Adrammelech, Anammelech, Nicrok, Nebo, Queen of Heaven, Rimmon and Tammuz.

Ezekiel 8 offers some details about various forms of worship of false gods which, in this case, took place in secret society style as it was done under the guise of worship within God's own Temple:

> ...the spirit lifted me up between the
> earth and the heaven, and brought
> me in the visions of God to
> Jerusalem, to the door of the inner

gate that looketh toward the north;
where was the seat of the image of
jealousy, which provoketh to
jealousy...the altar this image of
jealousy...

He said furthermore unto me, Son of
man, seest thou what they do? even
the great abominations that the house
of Israel committeth here, that I
should go far off from my sanctuary?
but turn thee yet again, and thou
shalt see greater abominations...

Then said he unto me, Son of man,
dig now in the wall: and when I had
digged in the wall, behold a door...
So I went in and saw; and behold
every form of creeping things, and
abominable beasts, and all the idols
of the house of Israel, pourtrayed
upon the wall round about.

And there stood before them seventy
men of the ancients of the house of
Israel, and in the midst of them stood
Jaazaniah the son of Shaphan, with
every man his censer in his hand;
and a thick cloud of incense went up.

Then said he unto me, Son of man,
hast thou seen what the ancients of
the house of Israel do in the dark,
every man in the chambers of his
imagery?...[at] the door of the gate of
the LORD'S house...sat women

weeping for Tammuz...[at] the inner
court of the LORD'S house, and,
behold, at the door of the temple of
the LORD, between the porch and
the altar, were about five and twenty
men, with their backs toward the
temple of the LORD, and their faces
toward the east; and they worshipped
the sun toward the east...

There are also many generic references to false gods
and/or idols such as within Exodus 12:12 which
states, "against all the gods of Egypt I will execute
judgment: I am the LORD" yet not naming any in
particular.

Amon

Amon tends to go unnoticed due to the very close relationship between two words so that the one is generally subsumed within the other.

The word *'amown* (Strong's H527) refers to a multitude, throng, crowd and populous as well as an artificer, architect and master workman.
It is found within Jeremiah 46:25, "The LORD of hosts, the God of Israel, saith; Behold, I will punish the multitude [*'amown*] of No, and Pharaoh, and Egypt, with their gods, and their kings; even Pharaoh, and all them that trust in him."

The same book employs it in 52:15 thusly, "Then Nebuzaradan the captain of the guard carried away captive certain of the poor of the people, and the residue of the people that remained in the city, and those that fell away, that fell to the king of Babylon, and the rest of the multitude [*'amown*]."

The only other place wherein it occurs is in Nahum 3:8, "Art thou better than populous [*'amown*] No, that was situate among the rivers, that had the waters round about it, whose rampart was the sea, and her wall was from the sea?"

Now, *'Amown* (Strong's H528) is the form which tends to go untranslated. It is aka *Amun*, means nourish or being faithful and refers to a deity that went from being localized to Thebes to becoming the head of the Egyptian pantheon.

One reason it is generally untranslated is that it is "used only as an adjunct of H4996 Amon (i.e. Ammon or Amn)" aka Amn-Re or Amon-Ra. This deity is generally depicted as a human body with a ram's head.

That the term is an adjunct of H4996 is another reason why it often goes unrecognized as *Amon* as the term is *No'* meaning "disrupting" and generally employed as the name of the Egypt's capital Thebes aka Diospolis.

This is the term "No" in the Jeremiah and Nahum texts and also appears thrice in Ezekiel 30 "And I will make Pathros desolate, and will set fire in Zoan, and will execute judgments in No. And I will pour my fury upon Sin, the strength of Egypt; and I will cut off the multitude of No. And I will set fire in Egypt: Sin shall have great pain, and No shall be rent asunder, and Noph shall have distresses daily."

This is why even though it appears in Jeremiah 46:25 it was not visible in the KJV quote above. Yet, it is not so much that it was not visible but that it is subsumed into the term "multitude" just as it is in the Nahum 3:8 term "populous."

Here are examples of how some translations handle it within the Jeremiah text:
NKJV "Amon of No, and Pharaoh" footnote on Amon reads, "A sun god"
HCSB, NET, NIV and NLT "Amon, the god of Thebes"
ESV, NASB and RSV "Amon of Thebes"
ASV, DBY, HNV and YLT "Amon of No"

Astaroth

'Ashtarowth (Strong's H6252) transliterated as *Ashtaroth, Astaroth*, etc. refers to *star* and was used as the name of a Canaanite, Sidonian deity. It is the plural of *'ashterah* (Strong's H6251) meaning ewe, flock, increase, young.

It was also used of a city in Bashan that was given to Manasseh; 1 Chronicles 11:44 refers to "Uzzia the Ashterathite." Gesenius's Hebrew-Chaldee Lexicon notes that it is "more fully called...'the horned Astartes'" which is *Ashtaroth-karnaim* (as in Genesis 14:5), "so called doubtless from a temple and statues of Astarte."

Judges 2:13, 10:6 and 1 Samuel 7:4, 12:10 refer to serving Baal or Baalim and Ashtaroth which is why they are viewed as a male and female deity duo.

1 Samuel 31:8-10 relates that "the Philistines...found Saul" dead "And they cut off his head, and stripped off his armour, and sent into the land of the Philistines round about, to publish it in the house of their idols, and among the people. And they put his armour in the house of Ashtaroth: and they fastened his body to the wall of Bethshan."

Baal

Ba'al (Strong's H1168 and G896) simply means *lord* and thus, has many applications such as the name of a town and a person. *Baalathbeer/Ba'alath Be'er* (Strong's H1192) was a saloon in Palestine— get it? "Beer," but I jest—actually, this is a feminine usage and mean "mistress of the well."

There is also *Bel* (Strong's H1078) which is the form when referring to the Babylonian Baal (for example, there is an apocryphal addition to the Book of Daniel titled, "Bel and the Dragon").

Within our context, it is a general manner whereby to refer to the main deity of the Phoenicians and Canaanites. The term is applied to other regional false gods such as *Baal-Peor*, *Baalpeor* or *Baal of Peor* (Strong's H1187) meaning lord of the gap and applied to a Moabitish deity (see Numbers 25:3, 25:5; Deuteronomy 4:3; Psalm 106:28 and Hosea 9:10).

Some information on the manners of worshipping Baal is as follows.
Numbers 22:41 refers to "the high places of Baal" with Jeremiah 19:5 adding that "They have built also the high places of Baal, to burn their sons with fire for burnt offerings unto Baal." Jeremiah 32:35 reiterates this with added details, "they built the high places of Baal, which are in the valley of the son of Hinnom, to cause their sons and their daughters to pass through the fire unto Molech" I will consider Molech in a section below.

1 Kings 18:26, 28 specifies that the priests of Baal sacrificed bullocks and "called on the name of Baal from morning even until noon, saying, O Baal, hear us. But there was no voice, nor any that answered. And they leaped upon the altar which was made…And they cried aloud, and cut themselves after their manner with knives and lancets, till the blood gushed out upon them."

We get two other details about Baal worship in 1 Kings 19:18 wherein the counter distinction between worshipers of Baal and those loyal to God is that the loyal are those with "knees which have not bowed unto Baal, and every mouth which hath not kissed him."

2 King 10:26 states that there were images in "the house of Baal." 2 Kings 23:4 notes "the vessels that were made for Baal."

2 Kings 17:16, 23:4 notes that Baal was worshipped in conjunction with or perhaps as a member of a pantheon whereby they "worshipped all the host of heaven, and served Baal." 23:5 specifies the burning of "incense unto Baal, to the sun, and to the moon, and to the planets, and to all the host of heaven" and Jeremiah 7:9, 11:13, 17 and 32:29 also references the incense rituals.
Jeremiah 2:8 notes that "the prophets prophesied by Baal."
Hosea 2:8 refers to "corn, and wine, and oil, and…silver and gold, which they prepared for Baal."
Romans 11:4 contains the only New Testament, Greek, reference which is a quotation of 1 Kings 19:18.

Lord of the Flies

Within the Old Testament *ba'al zebub* (Strong's H1176) combines *ba'al/lord* and *zebub* which, since it refers to flitting, was used as to refer to the insect, the fly (especially a stinging one such as a horse fly). Thus, *Baalzebub* is the *lord of the flies* and was the name of an Ekronite deity.

Within the New Testament *Beelzebub* (Strong's G954) is a term constructed from a Chaldee origin derived "by parody upon [H1176]); *dung god*; *Beelzebul*, a name of Satan" (brackets in original).

H1176 only appears within one text:
> And Ahaziah…was sick: and he sent messengers, and said unto them, Go, enquire of Baalzebub the god of Ekron whether I shall recover of this disease. But the Angel of the LORD said to Elijah the Tishbite, Arise, go up to meet the messengers of the king of Samaria, and say unto them…
>
> Is it not because there is not a God in Israel, that thou sendest to enquire of Baalzebub the god of Ekron? therefore thou shalt not come down from that bed on which thou art gone up, but shalt surely die (2 Kings 1).

G954 appears in more than one although most are parallel, reiterative, texts:

The disciple is not above his master,
nor the servant above his lord. It is
enough for the disciple that he be as
his master, and the servant as his
lord. If they have called the master of
the house Beelzebub, how much
more shall they call them of his
household? (Matthew 10:24-25).

Then was brought unto him one
possessed with a devil, blind, and
dumb: and he healed him, insomuch
that the blind and dumb both spake
and saw. And all the people were
amazed, and said, Is not this the son
of David?

But when the Pharisees heard it, they
said, This fellow doth not cast out
devils, but by Beelzebub the prince
[or chief] of the devils.
And Jesus knew their thoughts, and
said unto them, Every kingdom
divided against itself is brought to
desolation; and every city or house
divided against itself shall not stand:

And if Satan cast out Satan, he is
divided against himself; how shall
then his kingdom stand? And if I by
Beelzebub cast out devils, by whom
do your children cast them out?
therefore they shall be your judges
(Matthew 12, Mark 3 and Luke 11).

Belial

The Hebrew *beliya'al* (Strong's H1100) and Greek *belial* (Strong's G955) refer to being worthlessness, good for nothing, unprofitable, base fellow, wicked, ruin, destruction. The KJV translated thusly: Belial (16x), wicked (5x), ungodly (3x), evil (1x), naughty (1x), ungodly men (1x).

Wicked people are referred to as "children of Belial" in Deuteronomy 13:13; Judges 20:13; 1 Samuel 10:27; 1 Kings 21:13 (and also mentioned, "men of Belial"); 2 Chronicles 13:7.
Judges 19:22; 1 Samuel 2:12, 25:17; 2 Samuel 23:6; 1 Kings 21:10 have these personages described as "sons of Belial."
2 Samuel 16:7 and 20:1 has such a one as a "man of Belial."
When Eli thinks that Hannah, who was in prayer, was actually just drunk, she states the following in 1 Samuel 1:16, "Count not thine handmaid for a daughter of Belial."

Deuteronomy 15:9 has "thy wicked [*beliya'al*] heart." Job 34:18 has, "Is it fit to say to a king, Thou art wicked? [*beliya'al*] and to princes, Ye are ungodly?"
Psalm 101:3 states "I will set no wicked [*beliya'al*] thing before mine eyes."
Proverbs 6:12 refers to "A naughty [*beliya'al*] person, a wicked [in this case *'aven* Strong's H205] man."
Nahum 1:11 references "a wicked [*beliya'al*] counsellor" and verse 15 to "the wicked [*beliya'al*]" in general.

1 Samuel 30:22 refers to "the wicked [in this case *ra'* Strong's H7451] men and men of Belial."

1 Samuel 25:25 states, "Let not my lord, I pray thee, regard this man of Belial, even Nabal: for as his name is, so is he; Nabal is his name, and folly is with him: but I thine handmaid saw not the young men of my lord, whom thou didst send" this is because *Nabal* (Strong's H5037) means stupid, foolish, impious, wicked, etc.

2 Samuel 22:5 metaphorically references "the floods of ungodly men [*beliya'al*] made me afraid." Psalm 18:4 refers to "ungodly men [*beliya'al*]." Proverbs 16:27 refers to "An ungodly [*beliya'al*] man" and 19:28 to "An ungodly [*beliya'al*] witness."

Psalm 41:8 refers to "An evil [*beliya'al*] disease."

The only Greek usage is in 2 Corinthians 6:15 where it is claimed that it is employed as a term applied to Satan which may be the case but may also be its generic usage as defined above. Verses 14-16 read thusly:
> Be ye not unequally yoked together
> with unbelievers:
> for what fellowship hath
> righteousness with unrighteousness?
> and what communion hath light with
> darkness?
> And what concord hath Christ with
> Belial?
> or what part hath he that believeth
> with an infidel?

And what agreement hath the temple
of God with idols?
for ye are the temple of the living
God; as God hath said, I will dwell
in them, and walk in them; and I will
be their God, and they shall be my
people.

Chiun/Remphan

Kiyuwn/Chiun (Strong's H3594) may not be an actual idol but a reference to an image or pillar in general and therefore, was specifically employed for idolatrous "sacred pillars" for example. Yet, it may also refer to an Assyrian-Babylonian idol representing the planet Saturn or another planetary body.

Rhaiphan/Remphan (Strong's G4481) refers to "the shrunken" with the implication of something being lifeless.

Consider Amos 5:26 which is the only biblical reference to Chium, "But ye have borne the tabernacle of your Moloch and Chiun your images, the star of your god, which ye made to yourselves."

This is reiterated in Acts 7:43, "Yea, ye took up the tabernacle of Moloch, and the star of your god Remphan, figures which ye made to worship them: and I will carry you away beyond Babylon."

So, we have a reference to Moloch and Chiun and a supposed reiteration that lists them as Moloch and Remphan.

This is the reason that this section is titled, "Chiun/Remphan" since, as it turns out, the terms are interchangeable. Remphan is simply a Greek form of Chiun; Remphan is how the LXX translates the Amos 5 text.

Chemosh

Kemowsh/Chemosh (Strong's H3645) means subduer, conqueror, tamer and was a Moabite and Ammonite deity which was also identified with the above considered Baal-Peor, Baal-Zebub, Mars and Saturn.

We do not have much biblical information besides general references.

1 Kings 11:7 refers to "high place for Chemosh, the abomination of Moab" (also see 2 Kings 23:13).

Numbers 21:29 refers to the "people of Chemosh" meaning worshippers of or an indication that the term was employed of a locality.

Dagon

Dagown/Dagon (Strong's H1712) means *a fish* and was a Philistine deity of fertility depicted idolatrously as a humanoid form with the face and hands of a man yet, the tail of a fish.

Judges 16:23 notes that the Philistines "offer a great sacrifice unto Dagon their god."

1 Samuel 5:2-5 relates the following:
...the Philistines took the ark of God, they brought it into the house of Dagon, and set it by Dagon...early on the morrow, behold, Dagon was fallen upon his face to the earth before the ark of the LORD. And they took Dagon, and set him in his place again.

And when they arose early on the morrow morning, behold, Dagon was fallen upon his face to the ground before the ark of the LORD; and the head of Dagon and both the palms of his hands were cut off upon the threshold; only the stump of Dagon was left to him.

Therefore neither the priests of Dagon, nor any that come into Dagon's house, tread on the threshold of Dagon in Ashdod unto this day.

1 Chronicles 10 informs us that when the Philistines found King Saul dead "they took his head…and fastened his head in the temple of Dagon."

Marduk

The commonly termed *Marduk* (*Merodach* in the KJV) is *Merodak* (Strong's H4781) meaning *thy rebellion* and refers to the main Babylonian deity thus, it is aka Bel and many other names.

The only biblical reference to this particular name is in Jeremiah 50:2 which also employs the term Bel, "...Babylon is taken, Bel is confounded, Merodach is broken in pieces; her idols are confounded, her images are broken in pieces."

Molech

Molek generally transliterated as *Molech* or *Moloch* (Strong's H4432 and G3434) means *king* and is an Ammonite and Phoenician version of the Hebrew for *king* which is *melek* (Strong's H4428).

There are various references to child sacrifice to Molech which is termed "pass through the fire to Molech" (see Leviticus 18:21; 2 Kings 23:10; Jeremiah 32:35).

There are also references which specify the giving of "seed unto Molech" which is either another manner whereby to refer to children or some form of sexual ritual, see Leviticus 20:2-4 with verse 5 referring to those who "commit whoredom with Molech."

1 Kings 11:7 notes that "Solomon build an high place for Chemosh" whom I consider in a section above, "the abomination of Moab, in the hill that is before Jerusalem, and for Molech, the abomination of the children of Ammon."

The only New Testament reference is Acts 7:43, "Yea, ye took up the tabernacle of Moloch, and the star of your god Remphan, figures which ye made to worship them: and I will carry you away beyond Babylon."

Milcom

Malkam (Strong's H4445) transliterated as *Malcam,
Malcham, Milcom* is another term that derives from
melek and which means *great king.*

It is applied to an Ammonite and Phoenician deity
and it sometimes an aka for Molech. It appears as a
person's name in 1 Chronicles 8:9.

Otherwise, we are not given many details and
Micom is referenced amongst other Pagan deities
namely Ashtoreth and Chemosh (see 1 Kings 11:5,
33 and 2 Kings 23:13).

Nergal, Ashima, Nibhaz Tartak, Adrammelech and Anammelech

These six are listed together as they only appear once in the Bible and all within the same verse.

> And the men of Babylon made Succothbenoth, and the men of Cuth made Nergal, and the men of Hamath made Ashima,
> And the Avites made Nibhaz and Tartak, and the Sepharvites burnt their children in fire to Adrammelech and Anammelech, the gods of Sepharvaim (2 Kings 17:30-31).

Succothbenoth/Cukkowth benowth (Strong's H5524) literally means "the daughter's booth" and was the name of an Assyrian and/or Babylonian deity worshipped in Samaria.

Nergal (Strong's H5370) means "hero" and was an Assyria and Babylon deity worshipped by the Cuthites.

Ashima/'Ashiyma' (aka *Asima* and *Ashi'ma*) (Strong's H807) means "guiltiness: I will make desolate" and was a deity of Hamathites.

Whatever his sources were, the occultist Alphonse Louis Constant aka Eliphas Levi (1810-1875 AD) illustrated an idol he called *Azima*. This is somewhat of a mirror image of another illustration of Levi's which is called *Baphomet* about which the *The Royal Masonic Cyclopedia* states:

BAPHOMET.—Among the charges preferred against the Order of Knights Templar, for which Jacques de Molay suffered martyrdom, was that of worshipping an idol or image called Baphomet or Baphometus. Many discussions have arisen respecting this word. Maccoy considers it to have been a corruption of Mohammed; but when it is remembered that the very object of the Templar Order was to combat the faith of Islam, it is easy to see that such a view must be erroneous. Von Hammer suggests that it may have arisen from the two Greek words, βάφη μητις, *the baptism of wisdom*; and Nicolai suggests that the three heads, sometimes shown on the image, referred to the Trinity ; but it might be as well referred to Cerberus, as we have dog-headed divinities constantly in the Egyptian and Hellenic mysteries. It is curious that *bafa* is the Provençal for a falsehood.

That it was a Kabbalistical talisman is unquestionable, and was connected with the esoteric doctrines of Hermetic philosophy. It is very likely that an image embodying these doctrines may have existed, nor is it difficult to reconstruct its singular form, in itself essentially Masonic and universal.

Be it remembered that the Rabbis were the jealous custodians of the science of the Cabala or Kabbalah, and that their mystical form of reading would prevail in the terminology of that science. If the word be read in the Hebrew manner (that is, instead of BAPHOMET, read thus, TEMOHPAB), it is found to be an abbreviated cipher of the words, TEMpli Omnium Hominum Paces ABbas—"The father of the Temple, the universal peace of men," thus conveying in a phrase an appropriate and universal sentiment of a Masonic nature. It has been suggested that Baphomet is none other than the Ancient of Days or Creator. More cannot be said here without improperly revealing what we are bound to hele, conceal, and never reveal.[2]

L: *Azima*, R: *Baphomet*

Nibhaz (Strong's H5026) means "the barker" represented by an idol in the form of a dog, was a deity of the Avites.

Tartaq/Tartak (Strong's H8662) means "prince of darkness" and was a deity of the Avites of Samaria which was represented by an idol in the form of a donkey.

'Adrammelek/Adrammelech (Strong's H152) means "honour of the king," "Adar is prince" (or *king* I would assume due to *melek/melech*) and/or "Adar is Counsellor, Decider."
'Anammelek/Anammelech (Strong's H6048) means "image of the king."
These were deities of the Sepharvites and Assyrians. Adrammelech is also the name of the son and murderer of Sennacherib as per 2 Kings 19:37 and Isaiah 37:38.

Nicrok

Nicrok (Strong's H5268) means *the great eagle* and was the term for an idold of Nineveh amd Babylon which had the appearance of a human form with an eagle's head.

The only mention is in passing in 2 Kings 19:37 and reiterated in Isaiah 37:38 when Sennacherib, the king of Assyria, "was worshipping in the house of Nisroch his god" when "Adrammelech and Sharezer his sons smote him with the sword...And Esarhaddon his son reigned in his stead."

Nebo

Nebo (*Nĕbow* Strong's H5015) is a variously employed term which is probably of foreign derivation and used in the Bible for a foreign prophet in Isaiah 46:1,

> Bel boweth down, Nebo stoopeth,
> their idols were upon the beasts, and
> upon the cattle: your carriages were
> heavy loaden; they are a burden to
> the weary beast.

It is also the name of a Moabite city likely located at or near *Mount Nebo* and a city in Judah whence came, likely Benjamite, families when they returned from Babylonian captivity with Zerubbabel. And, it refers to where Moses died (east of the Jordan).

Yet, it is included here as this is also the name of a Babylonian deity which was viewed as the celestial scribe by Chaldeans and ancient Arabians.

Thus, this was the god who presided over learning and letters as the later Hermes would do for Greek, Mercury also for the Chaldeans as well as the Assyrians, and Thoth for the Egyptians.

Gesenius' Hebrew-Chaldee Lexicon informs us that "we find it attested by the proper names which have this name at the beginning, as *Nebuchadnezzar, Nebushasban*...and also those mentioned by classic writers, *Nabonebus, Nabonassar, Naburisanus, Nabonabus*, etc."

For all of its usages—*Finding Nebo*—see Numbers 32:3, 38, 33:47; Deuteronomy 32:49, 34:1; 1 Chronicles 5:8; Ezra 2:29, 10:43; Nehemiah 7:33; Isaiah 15:2, 46:1; Jeremiah 48:1, 22.

Queen of Heaven

The term *Queen of Heaven* is *Meleketh Shamayim* (Strong's H4446 and H8064) and is specifically referenced by Jeremiah from whom we get quite a bit of detail.

Chapter 7 states:

> Will ye steal, murder, and commit adultery, and swear falsely, and burn incense unto Baal, and walk after other gods whom ye know not; And come and stand before me in this house [God's Temple], which is called by my name, and say, We are delivered to do all these abominations?...
>
> The children gather wood, and the fathers kindle the fire, and the women knead their dough, to make cakes to the queen of heaven, and to pour out drink offerings unto other gods, that they may provoke me to anger...

Chapter 44 offers additional information as the people reply as follows to Jeremiah's rebuking of their idolatry:

> As for the word that thou hast spoken unto us in the name of the Lord, we will not hearken unto thee. But we will certainly do whatsoever thing goeth forth out of our own mouth, to burn incense unto the

queen of heaven, and to pour out
drink offerings unto her…burn
incense to the queen of heaven, and
to pour out drink offerings unto
her…we make her cakes to worship
her…

Rimmon

Rimmon (Strong's H7417) means *pomegranate* and besides being employed as the name of a rocky cliff and a city, it is also used with reference to "the deity of wind, rain, and storm, worshipped by the Syrians of Damascus."

Thus, it appears in 2 Kings 5 wherein Naaman, who was the captain of the host of the king of Syria, stated the following after having been healed by God:

> In this thing the LORD pardon thy servant, that when my master goeth into the house of Rimmon to worship there, and he leaneth on my hand, and I bow myself in the house of Rimmon: when I bow down myself in the house of Rimmon, the LORD pardon thy servant in this thing.

Tammuz

Tamuz (Strong's H8542) only appears in Ezekiel 8:14:

> Then he brought me to the door of
> the gate of the LORD'S house which
> was toward the north; and, behold,
> there sat women weeping for
> Tammuz.

This was in reference to a false front of worshipping in God's temple whilst actually performing Pagan rites. The term means "sprout of life" and refers to a Sumerian and Phoenician deity of food or vegetation.

Demons as the Paranormal Theory of Everything

Paranormal is a term that is variously employed within our common parlance. The prefix *para* refers to something side by side of something else; such in *para*llel, *para*legal (one who works side by side with a lawyer), etc.

*Para*normal refers to the concept of a reality that exists side by side of that which is generally termed our four dimensions (three spatial and plus time) and thus by extension refers to something that is impossible to explain; at least within a materialistic framework.

With *paranormal* being such a wide term there is much to which it is applied such as ghosts, extra-terrestrial aliens and their UFOs, gods and goddesses of various sorts: telepathy (mind to mind communication), necromancy (communicating with the dead such as is done by psychic spirit channeling mediums), telekinesis (moving objects without touching them) and much, much more.

Of course, much more could be included but this a rough sketch. These may be broken down into two categories as follows: 1) Ghosts, aliens, UFOs, gods/goddesses and 2) Telepathy, necromancy, telekinesis.

1) Ghosts, Aliens, UFOs, Gods/Goddesses

Interestingly, and tellingly, the "appearance" of ghosts, aliens, UFOs, gods/goddesses could be "physical" or some form of manifestation but need not be.

In other words: Ghosts may be seen as apparitions but may also manifest invisibly (as in the case of poltergeists, troublesome spirits, which move things around but are not necessarily seen).

Aliens may appear physically (in order to experiment on people, etc.) but also send messages telepathically without being present—and even while present they seem to prefer, or are restricted to, this method.

This denotes the difference between *abductees* (who experience the physical side of it) and *contactees* and/or *experiences* (whose experiences may be strictly telepathic).

UFO is one of those catch all terms as it literally and simply means **U**nidentified **F**lying **O**bject.

Thus, a distant bird could be a UFO if you identify that it is flying but cannot determine what it is.

Within the alien context, UFO is another manner whereby to refer to spaceships, alien craft.

While some of these appear to be nuts and bolts, in a manner of speaking, 3-D vehicles, others appear to be globes/spheres/orbs of light/energy (still others are the government's secret experimental craft).

As with aliens; gods/goddesses—and for that matter *ascended masters, light beings, spirit guides*, etc.—

can appear physically or communicate via telepathy.

2) Telepathy, Necromancy, Telekinesis.

These abilities are interpreted variously as everything from the claim that these *superpower*-like abilities are somehow acquired by a select few to the claim that we all have these as latent or dormant and perfectly *normal* human abilities which, for some or another reason, are not generally accessed and employed.

Obviously, categories 1) and 2) interact since ghosts, aliens, gods/goddesses employ telepathy and telekinesis and communicating with ghosts is a form of necromancy. This is one reason why these are all categorized as paranormal.

Demons are disembodied intelligences much like our mind is the software and our brain is our hardware (which is why they seek hardware to wear via possession). These beings are around us and know much about us.

Moreover, by merely our fallen natures we are susceptible to them and when we engage in occult practices we open the doors wide for them to enter (part of the apparently litigious nature of possession).

Involvement in the occult leads deeper and deeper into the occult; even if, and especially when, the demons decide to play nice in a PR stunt whereby the pretend to be benevolent guides, dearly departed ones, etc.

The bottom line is that demons may be around us and our families for generations and thus, can repeat something that you think no one but your deceased loved ones could possibly know—play acting of sorts and relaying information which was gathered about a now deceased person.

This also ties in to ghosts which may simply be demonic manifestations, at whatever level.

As they are familiar with families, have even heard secret conversations, know that the lost set of keys fell behind the stove, know what good ol' aunty Ethel (or, in this case, aunty *Ether*) sounded like, etc. they can pretend to be any family member as they know much about them.

Demons appear to be able to cause certain manifestations of phenomena which is how we end up with light shows such as globes/spheres/orbs as well as apparitions (some of those are actually none but natural phenomena such as "ball lightning").

Fig. 2. — Le globe de feu dans la salle.

19th century engraving depicting ball lightning

"Mind reading," by any other name and implanting a thought into someone else's brain could be one *familiar spirit-demon* conveying information to another.

Yet, on a more *physical* level it may be done by tapping into someone's frequency, as we all exude an electrical frequency, much like we can tap into *invisible* radio waves by attuning our radio's antenna to a certain frequency.

These are speculations but seem to be the answer to the claims of psychic mediums, mind readers, channelers, etc. Granting that there are some such personages who are utter frauds.

And yet, some appear to be part fraud and partly in actual contact with what they term the spirits of deceased humans and some appear to be in conscious contact with spirits.

135

The point being that familiar spirit-demons make for a good answer to the psychic medium issue. Such personages open themselves up to contact with well, whatever may be *out there* and familiar spirit-demons are more than pleased to make contact.

When it comes down to it, the majority of alien messages are nothing that has not been stated 1,001 time already in New Age literature (much which comes from psychic spirit channeling mediums via ascended masters and aliens in the first place).

Matthew 12:43-45 (reiterated in Luke 11:24-26) notes that there are "spirits more wicked" than others. Thus, perhaps the mellower spirits are assigned secretarial type roles and observe families and record, in whatever manner, information about them.
However, the more wicked ones may be the ones that act out in the form of violent possession and poltergeist activities.

According to the Bible there are disembodies beings known variously as *demons* which are categorized as principalities, powers, etc. (see the *Angel Category* section of *What Does the Bible Say About Angels?* and the sections herein on demons, devils and spirits).

Appendix: On Extra-Terrestrial Alien Messages

When it comes to extra-terrestrial or extra-dimensional or perhaps para-terrestrial or para-dimensional alien messages we must ask one *what* question about their messages and two *how* questions: 1) what are their messages, 2) how are the messages are received and 3) how their messages are to be turned into plans that are subsequently to be put into place and carried out.

This will be a succinct and generally generic review of the main points so that you may discern them when you encounter them.
For details, see my book *Fifty Shades of Gray Aliens*.

There are very many reported forms of, supposed alleged, aliens ranging from big headed, big eyed and small bodied grays/greys (some of which are said to be just as skinny but quite tall) to Nordics who are human in form, having blue eyes and blond hair and from short hooded gorilla-like faced beings to reptilians and many more.

What?

When it comes down to it, regardless of the variation in terminology and details, the message is the same whether it comes from aliens, spirit guides, higher beings, ascended maters, etc.

The message is that we humans are destroying the Earth and ourselves. As we are part of some great cosmic community our actions affect beings who are not Earth-dwellers. And often it is said that we negatively affect the Earth itself with the view of the Earth as a living entity (*Gaia*, etc.).

The follow up from the observation that humans are causing such great harm is that we must come together and thus unite so as to achieve global change. We must set aside our outdated and destructive theologies, we must set aside our outdated and destructive governments, we must set aside our outdated and destructive social mores, etc.

How?, 1

As to *how* the messages are received; it varies quite a bit. Nordics, for example, simply land their spacecraft, come across someone and speak to them vocally. Others, such as grays/greys communicate *telepathically* and this seems to be the preferred method for most aliens.

This, of course, is very convenient because it means that they can communicate to, and through, humans even from vast distances (and other points in chronology) and thus, without the necessity of being physically present. Also, this does not require them to travel and so we end up with the difference between *contactees, abductees, experiencers*, etc. In other words, one need not see or board a spacecraft nor see an alien in order to communicate with them.

This leads to the odd correlation between spirit channeling mediums and alien channelers; those who claim to channel the spirits of the deceased and those who claim to channel aliens do the very same things (and involvement in the occult is step one).

They both *open themselves up* to receive whatever happens to be out there and there are certainly beings *floating around* out there looking for, metaphorical, neon signs on people's heads that say "Come in, we're open."

How?, 2

The second *how* is (having set such outdated and destructive beliefs and practices aside) how such entities propose that we accomplish such changes. Again, regardless of terminology or details, it all leads to the same place; a new world order—by any other name.

This is because the ultimate answer, the *how*, is for us to adopt a one world religion consisting of alien theology—which is always impersonal "pantheism," meaning that there is no personal God but only what is variously known as energy, prana, qi, ki, chi, vril, the force, etc.

The *how* is that we must adopt a new governmental system, a one world government. And we must also adopt a new morality as traditional family units (and by extension clans, tribes, nations, etc.) only cause division and hording of goods.

Along with this—and again this is the same whether it comes from the happy faced New Age or the frowny faced Nazis—comes the concept that human population size must be drastically reduced and that vast numbers of people will be done away with. The

Nazis had a very physical and hands on approach while the New Age conceptualizes it as people being taken off the Earth by some UFO related or metaphysical (or, both) event.

In short, always read between the lines because there is a reason that, on the ground level, New Agers, Nazis, Transhumanists, magickians, mystery religions, secret societies and many, many more agree. They all seek to establish a new world order.

Index

Endnotes

[1] Here is a list of the Bibles to which I appeal: Aramaic Peshitta: AP, American Standard Version: ASV, Darby Bible: DBY, Dead Sea Scrolls: DSS, English Standard Version: ESV, Geneva Bible with Notes: GBN, Holoman Christian Standard Bible: HCSB, Hebrew Names Version: HNV, Jewish Publication Society: JPS, New American Bible: NAB, New American Standard Bible: NASB, New International Version: NIV, New King James Version: NKJV, New Living Translation: NLT, Revised Standard Version: RSV, Targum Onkelos: TONK, Targum Pseudo-Jonathan: TPJ, World English Bible: WEB, Young's Literal Translation: YLT and Septuagint: LXX.

[2] Kenneth Mackenzie, *The Royal Masonic Cyclopedia* (1877 AD – The Aquarian Press, 1987 AD ed.)

Made in the USA
San Bernardino, CA
06 December 2018